Sourcing Ideas for Textile Design

Researching Colour, Surface, Structure, Texture and Pattern

Second edition

BLOOMSBURY VISUAL ARTS

LONDON • NEW YORK • OXFORD • NEW DELHI • SYDNEY

BLOOMSBURY VISUAL ARTS
Bloomsbury Publishing Plc
50 Bedford Square, London, WC1B 3DP, UK
1385 Broadway, New York, NY 10018, USA

BLOOMSBURY, BLOOMSBURY VISUAL ARTS and the Diana logo are
trademarks of Bloomsbury Publishing Plc

First edition published by AVA Publishing SA, 2012
This second edition published by Bloomsbury Visual Arts,
first published in Great Britain 2020

A catalogue record for this book is available from the British Library.

Library of Congress Cataloging-in-Publication Data
Names: Steed, Josephine, author. | Stevenson, Frances, author.
Title: Sourcing ideas for textile design : researching colour, surface, structure,
texture and pattern / Josephine Steed, Frances Stevenson.
Description: New York : Bloomsbury, 2020. | Series: Basics textile design |
Includes bibliographical references.
Identifiers: LCCN 2019037352 | ISBN 9781350077638 (paperback) | ISBN 9781350077645 (pdf)
Subjects: LCSH: Textile design. | Textile design–Case studies. | Textile designers–Interviews. |
Textile design–Research. | Textile industry.
Classification: LCC TS1475 .S722 2020 | DDC 677/.022–dc23
LC record available at https://lccn.loc.gov/2019037352

ISBN: PB: 978-1-3500-7763-8
          ePDF: 978-1-3500-7764-5

Typeset by Integra Software Services Pvt. Ltd.
Printed and bound in India

To find out more about our authors and books visit www.bloomsbury.com
and sign up for our newsletters.

0 Work in progress by Karen Nicol.

5

Creating Textile Outcomes 125

Textile design is an extensive subject that covers a wealth of traditional design contexts, from enriching our clothing to decorating our homes, workplaces and public spaces. Due to this breadth, textile design overlaps and also drives innovation within many other areas, including fashion, jewellery, architecture and product design.

With the development of new technologies, together with increased digital possibilities, the scope for textile designers today has widened considerably where the subject has expanded and overlaps into new areas of both individual and collaborative practices. Equally, the responsibilities of the textile designer have changed where an awareness of ecological and **sustainability** issues concerning the textile industry are paramount.

Whatever the context, and however the creative journey, going from concept to final design begins with a process of researching and gathering ideas from which to produce inspirational textile outcomes. An understanding of the research and ideas-gathering stage is essential.

This book aims to introduce the fundamental techniques required for this crucial part of the textile design process.

Throughout the book, visual examples and a number of short exercises help to fully equip the reader for their own creative experimentation. We hope you will find the book both informative and inspiring, as well as a helpful companion throughout your creative research and design practice.

> **I like to challenge ways of looking at things.**
> Hanna Wearing

1 **The Dries Van Noten marble print coats designed for winter 2018 have been hand crafted using the Turkish craft of Ebru marbling. The application of colour onto cloth is applied through splattering and brushing colour pigment onto an oily water solution.**

1

What is Textile Design?

Typically, the textile designer's major role is within colour, pattern and fabric **aesthetics**. This is now evolving to include a wider range of opportunities. Through developments including digital technologies and social media platforms, consumers and clients today can be involved in the design process from the start through online user-generated content.

Many of the methods used to do this are similar to those used within other creative disciplines, but the textile designer views and analyses the world through a very specific lens.

To help us understand this, this chapter will look at textile design as a discipline and at how it differs from other creative subjects. We will explore the different opportunities available to a graduate in textile design and discover the career paths within textiles. Overall, this chapter will introduce you to textile design and how textile design is explored visually through material investigation, colour analysis, craftsmanship, surface detail, textual qualities and pattern-making.

2 **Detail from Manish Arora's work demonstrates how different textile processes form such an integral part of the fashion industry. The 'motifs' form a dominant part of the overall piece and demonstrate how the arrangement of colour and pattern can convey a unique overall composition.**

What makes Textile Design Different from other Disciplines?

Textile design generally refers to the process of creating knitted, woven, printed and mixed-media fabrics for multiple contexts. The textile designer needs to be able to understand how to produce a design for a particular fabric type and suitability for a given purpose known as a context – usually for clothing (fashion and specialist wearables), or for a particular space (an environment or specific place). Designers also require a good understanding of **contemporary** design issues as well as colour and trend awareness in order that their designs are relevant for their end purpose.

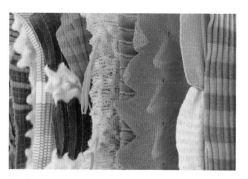

3a **Student knitted samples. This student uses a variety of knitted construction techniques and yarns to create these playful colourful and textural samples.**

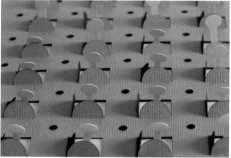

3c **Student mixed-media sample. This student is inspired by modular systems to create laser-cut neoprene samples for interiors.**

3b **Wallace and Sewell woven scarves.**

3d **Student print samples. This student uses pigment and collaged foils to create abstract large-scale interior pieces.**

Textile designers develop skills and knowledge specific to one of these areas: knit, weave, print or **mixed media**. Each one of these specialisms requires a different type of technical knowledge, as well as different types of equipment and materials. They all encompass a broad range of design processes and approaches. Printed textile designers design surface pattern. Woven and knitted (or 'constructed') textile designers tend to create a fabric from scratch, selecting fibres and yarns at the beginning of the process. Textile designers also often employ other techniques to create fabric (often referred to as mixed-media techniques). Mixed media is often used in conjunction with either knit, weave or print, but is also a **craft** of making in its own right. Digital fabrications are now also available to create textiles, such as laser cutting and **rapid prototyping** techniques using two- and three-dimensional **computer-aided design** (CAD).

What is Context?

In conjunction with these visual considerations, textile designers must also explore **contextual** research to consider who their designs are for and how they will be made.

Context can be described as the framework that supports an idea or concept as a set of considerations that the design work will focus around. Context is about understanding the specific requirements of those you are designing for and how to respond to their needs within your design work. Examples of this within textile design may include sustainable fashion, design for a public space, design for a major retailer. Understanding context ensures that your final design work is relevant to its intended outcome.

Definitions

A number of definitions can help to explain the main parameters and contexts of a textile designer:

Textile Design – Textile designers work within a **commercial** framework where they respond to certain constraints, for example costs, client, specific function and purpose. They work primarily within two defined areas:

BODY Used within the textile design industry, 'body' refers to fabric design for fashion, accessories and clothing, incorporating issues such as health, well-being and smart wearables.

SPACE Textile design for 'space' incorporates textile and material design for the built environment, interiors, furnishings and transport.

Definition of Textile Processes

PRINT A mark or impression made in or on a surface using pressure or chemical reaction.

4a The printing process involves placing screens onto the cloth, which is laid out onto a flat table, then pulling the ink through the screen using a squeegee.

WOVEN TEXTILES Fabric is made by interlacing the threads of the weft and the warp on a loom.

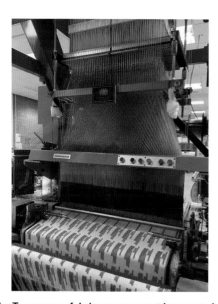

4c To weave a fabric a warp must be created, usually on a frame or a loom. Yarns are then woven across the warp threads (the weft) to create the cloth.

KNITTING Crochet or lace is created using yarn that interlocks, producing consecutive loops called stitches.

4b This image shows an example of hand machine knitting using a double-bed knitting machine.

MIXED-MEDIA TEXTILES Mixed-media textiles encompass many techniques, such as stitch and embroidery, pleating, bonding and dyeing, to name just a few.

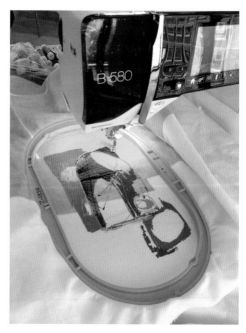

4d This image shows work being created through digital embroidery. The marks for the drawing are being translated through stitch.

What are the Concerns and Considerations of the Textile Designer?

Technological advances and changes in consumer lifestyles, together with sustainability and environmental issues, are now major factors for the designer to consider. Throughout the design process an awareness of these issues is imperative for designers as the design industry is now required to responsibly consider where its materials originate from. Some of the questions that textile designers are now being asked to consider include:

- Were all materials ethically sourced?
- Where did they come from?
- What processes were used in their production?
- Can waste be reduced?
- What is the lifecycle of the product and can it be recycled?
- What are the long-term implications of your design?
- Is it biodegradable?

Ethical and environmental considerations challenge designers in new ways. Many designers today recognize their responsibilities in reducing waste and their impact on the environment. Design companies are increasingly using their environmental and ethical policies as part of their marketing and branding strategies to encourage consumers to buy.

5 The Copenhagen fashion summit meets annually to discuss sustainability issues with the textile supply chain.

Exercise – Observation and Awareness

Think about the textile methods of print, knit, weave and mixed media. Take a look around you and note how textiles have been used in your environment. Consider the work that has gone into each stage of the process in order to arrive at the finished product you see now. Make a note also of all the ethical and sustainability considerations for each stage.

What are the Occupations?

Textile design education provides opportunities for a variety of different career paths. Previously, we mentioned the distinctive design and technical differences of knit, weave, print and mixed media. Following on from this, we will now look at some of the design professions available after specializing in textile design.

The Textile Industry

When using the term 'textile industry' we are usually referring to the commercial manufacturing side of textiles. The term also incorporates all the subsidiary businesses working together within clothing and fabric manufacture. These include spinners, dyers, fabric finishers, trimming manufacturers and accessory producers – essentially all those providing a service or product for the production of textiles, including technical textiles for a range of industries from fashion to aeronautical. As a textile designer, you may work as a commercial designer for a large manufacturer or as a freelance designer **commissioned** to design a range for a particular company or brand. Whatever area of textiles you ultimately choose to work within, you will need to understand how the textile industry operates.

Textile courses today have well-established links with textile companies, providing a range of industry-related opportunities to gain an insight into professional work. Student projects and placements are perfect for gaining experience within the industry, and can lead to further design work or future job offers.

6 Jobs in the textile industry can include spinners, dyers, fabric finishers, trimmings and accessory producers. An understanding of the textile industry is essential for all textile designers.

Craft Maker

Textile craft can be used to describe a wide range of textiles, including one-off, commissioned or limited-edition pieces. Craft makers often work independently but frequently exhibit and sell work collectively and pool resources by sharing communal studio spaces. They have a highly developed understanding of their particular niche market, developed over many years of refining their practice. Craft is such an expansive subject but can include makers working within the applied arts, textiles for exhibition, **conceptual** textiles, 3D textiles, accessories and clothing. Major craft fairs are held annually across continents, attracting international attention and opportunities to sell and interact with buyers.

> **Craft is an extraordinary thing of wonder; encompassing skill, creativity, artistry and emotion with thought, process, practicality and function. It is one of the purest forms of expression.**
> Tricia Guild

7 **Jane Keith is a Scottish printed-textile designer who produces exquisite hand-printed cloth from her studio in Fife. Jane works on cashmere, wools and silks using vibrant colours inspired from the Scottish landscapes.**

Studio Designer

Working within a studio is undoubtedly the preferred working environment for most designers. The term 'studio' immediately alludes to creativity and experimentation, portraying a strong identity of a particular designer or company. But there are many different types of textile design studio. Designers working within commercial design agencies sell fabric or paper designs to a broad range of potential clients, ranging from high-end fashion houses to well-known high-street brands. Most fashion and interior companies also have their own in-house design team. Many design agencies will showcase their studio's designs at international fairs such as Première Vision, the world's largest clothing fabric fair in Paris.

8 The Premiere Vision Textiles Trade Fair supplies the international fashion and textiles industry with new fabrics and accessories. It is held twice a year in Paris and students are welcome on the specific 'student visit days'.

Yarn Designer

Often overlooked but essential areas for textile design are, of course, yarns and fibres. These need to be designed by yarn spinners in order to be applicable for a given fabric design and purpose. Often, the main focus for the design of yarn is colour, where the colour prediction industry plays a vital role. Yarn design also includes developing textured specialist yarns and fibre blends. These specialist yarns are often produced specifically for the knitting and weaving industry and also for the amateur textile market, such as hand-knitters and craft enthusiasts. Yarn spinners will exhibit their yarn collections at trade yarn and spinners' fairs such as Pitti Filati in Florence, Italy. This enables yarn manufacturers to showcase and sell their yarn collections primarily to the knitting and weaving industry.

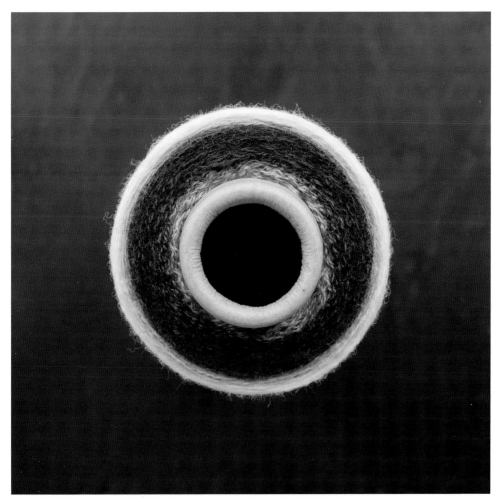

9 **Yarn designed by Mhairi Abbas. Mhairi dyes her yarns before knitting them into exquisite fashion accessories.**

Digital Designer

Computer-aided design and manufacture, also known as CAD/CAM, is today a well-integrated part of the textile industry. Textile designers combine hand craft with CAD technology to produce their designs, which can then be reproduced on compatible computer-operated machinery. Many CAD agencies today employ textile designers to use digital technology as a creative tool to realize their design ideas. Design work can then be digitally transferred anywhere in the world to be manufactured. Individual textile designers also use technology for a number of other purposes: to engage with their customers through social media networks and forums, through their own individual websites and through **e-commerce** websites for collective artists and designers.

10 **Digitally designed artwork can be directly printed onto a specially coated synthetic or man-made cloth enabling the designer to have a photographic reproduction of their work onto fabric.**

Fashion Forecaster

Fashion-**forecasting** companies primarily provide the fashion and textile industry with information on proposed key styles and looks for the future. They usually work two to three years in advance. This time-frame is vital in order to supply the textile and fashion industry, from yarn manufacturers to high-street retailers, with the themes, colours and styles to work on for the coming seasons. Textile designers are well equipped to work within this creative environment. Often, designers are asked to produce fabrics on a given theme or to work directly on collating information on future trends.

Colour Predictor

Colour prediction is closely related to fashion forecasting, and the two often go hand in hand. Colour is an essential element of fashion and textile design, and getting it right is a highly specialized job. This will be discussed in depth in Chapter 5. More and more industries are today using colour prediction information as design becomes the main focus for consumers. The design of our mobile phones, computers, the cars we drive and even the layout and colours used within shopping centres, are all carefully considered using colour analysis and prediction data.

CURVE SHAPED SLEEVES

KENTA MATSUSHIGE FALL/WINTER 2016

11 This student bases their research for fashion on a love of Japanese costume and contemporary architecture.

What are the Distinct Differences between Textile Design and Textile Art?

In terms of materials, textile design and textile art are closely related where they both use yarns, fibres and fabrics together with processes of weave, embroidery and surface, to name but a few. The difference between them lies more in their intention and constraints. Textile design tends to be about production, function and context. Textile art refers to fine-art considerations and one-off pieces where hand making and the artist's conceptual ideas are the main consideration. The two often blur within designer-maker practices as textile craft, where the maker's aesthetics and functional use are closely linked and the work may be made in small production runs. However, craftsmanship is usually central to both definitions.

Definitions

A number of definitions can help to explain the considerations for a textile artist:

Textile Art Textile artists work within a less confined commercial framework where their personal ideas and concepts are expressed through textile materials and processes. They work primarily within the following defined areas:

EXPRESSION The textile artist expresses their creative ideas through textile materials where the intended outcome is for visual display within a gallery or museum. The curation of the work is often a significant consideration where they may have been commissioned to respond to a particular place or context.

CONCEPT For a textile artist the concept behind the work is an important aspect of the final piece. Here the planning and decisions are realized before the work is made and the final work is a manifestation of their conceptual thinking.

NARRATIVE This is where an account of something, for example a story or poem, which can then be used to conjure up visual references and imagery.

12 A student ideas board showing design development. The student is working to a design brief and the image shows their material and contextual considerations for possible design outcomes.

13 Lucy Orta's *Refuge Wear* examines textiles and clothing within the urban environment. Her work addresses concerns regarding displaced communities.

14 Faig Ahmed uses the traditional craft of rug weaving with its Islamic geometry and decorative motifs to create textile art that questions our continually changing existence. His work is crafted beautifully to convey the essence of the traditional rug through the richness of colour and texture in his final pieces. He brings together art concepts with craftsmanship.

Textile artist Freddie Robins is well known for her playful, witty and subversive knitted textiles. She uses the soft materials of knitting to tell stories, which in other mediums may otherwise seem macabre. In her piece 'Knitted Homes of Crime', tea cosies are knitted to represent the British homes of women who have killed, or the houses in which they have killed. 'I've always been obsessed with murder and what makes people feel they could kill, when for most of us that sort of behaviour is so outside the moral code', she explains.

> **Freddie Robins offers a challenge to the notion of knitting as a passive, benign activity. Robins brings conformity to subversion, setting knitting not as an activity of safety and comfort-production, but rather as a series of actions and processes through which identity and subjectivity can be formed and expressed. Robins upsets notions of utilitarianism in favour of artistic expressionism, function, and form in favour of conceptual rigor. In so doing she rejects craft-art arguments as irrelevant and misplaced borderlines.**
> Catherine Dormor, Artist, Researcher and Lecturer, 2013

15 Freddie Robins' *Knitted Homes of Crime* uses the non-threatening tea cosy as a metaphor for exploring controversial issues within society.

'Flower Head – Narcissistic Butterfly' by artist Michael Brennand-Wood, conceptually references the implied relationship between the floral and human head. Each individual embroidered flower has at its centre a human face, preserved at the end of a flexible wire. A bunch, or cast, of political and media characters. Sculpturally the form refers to the exotic, tiered pincushions into which hatpins were once stored. The embroidered flower is a twentieth-century snapshot, analogous to a preserved butterfly, in a museum case, a reflection of someone who has ceased to exist. I was also interested in the term 'pinhead', a derogatory critique of certain people in society, in this context; pinhead is deliberately ambiguous, referring to both people and the preservation of insects. Our leaders, those people who represent us, have an unfortunate sense of their own self-importance, a desire to be seen and constantly photographed at their best; the mirror is a literal reflection of their narcissism and our fascination with other people's media lives.

16 FLOWER HEAD – NARCISSISTIC BUTTERFLY 2005 © Michael Brennand Wood

What is the Textile Design Process?

Within textile design there is clear and helpful process that can guide you through each stage in order to complete your project. Working through this process is important as it allows you to explore your ideas in depth and drive your thinking at all times in order to achieve the most creative outcome. Understanding this process will essentially strengthen your concept and final outcome and will help to find an idea worth exploring or refine an idea that you already have.

The process diagram explains the key areas within textile design. Each area is interconnected to demonstrate how you can move between areas to reach the final design. It is important to note that these areas overlap continually, and activities like drawing and contextual research are central to more than one area. However, we have simplified how you can work through each area in order to explain the types of activity that usually take place. We believe that engaging with this process will help you interpret information and form your own independent way of thinking.

There are three key areas that are central to the textile design process. They are IDEA, DEVELOP and CREATE.

Create: Produce your final designs that are fit for purpose. This stage involves making pieces to a professional standard.

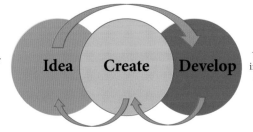

Idea: Be open-minded at this stage. Explore your idea through contextual and visual research.

Develop: Find and record visual information. Look for inspirational textures, colours and patterns. Start material investigation at this stage.

17 This diagram shows the three stages of textile design referred to in this book as IDEA, DEVELOP, CREATE. Ultimately, the stages are interlinked and fluid as designers move from one stage to the next and back again.

IDEA

At the beginning of a project, it is important to be open-minded and receptive to new ideas and different ways of thinking. You might have a 'big' area that you would like to explore further to find a particular focus within, or you may start with a smaller focused idea that needs more in-depth investigation. At this early stage, you should explore a broad range of areas and thoughts around your idea. This is an exciting phase where you can really think outside of the box, so stretch the boundaries of the idea by considering every potential avenue to explore. This first stage involves extensive contextual research to help refine your area, and drawings and sketches to help you think things through and provide visual information that can be used for design development.

DEVELOP

The DEVELOP stage focuses primarily on visual research and how you process this information through further investigation. At this stage it is important to find and record visual information related to your IDEA phase through your drawing, as this will provide you with inspirational textures, colours, structures and patterns that you can 'play' with before you start material exploration. 'Playing' with the information in your sketchbook/workbook is important in order to transform the initial drawings into new information that can be explored through textile materials. Material investigation is a fundamental part of development as you hone your skills in various processes and make **prototype** samples that can be developed further. The DEVELOP stage is the most in-depth stage and takes the most time, effort and dedication. This is where the eureka moments usually happen!

CREATE

This stage of creating exciting new textiles is wholly dependent on the thoroughness of your IDEA and DEVELOP stage. Material samples will be created as a collection where they come together and complement one another within your context. You will have trialled a variety of techniques and colour **palettes** and so on in the first two stages, and the final work will reflect the previous exploration and decision-making that you have made through the IDEA and DEVELOP stages. The final designs should combine skilful handling of materials, and a good level of craftsmanship with a 'fit for purpose' context. This stage is about making the final pieces and communicating and presenting your work to a professional standard.

Chapter 2 will discuss each of these stages, IDEA, DEVELOP and CREATE, in more detail.

> **You can find inspiration in everything; if you can't find it then you're not looking properly.**
> Paul Smith

18 A student studio display board exploring a range of both primary and contextual research analysing lines and stripe patterns.

19 Student knitwear piece. This shows the final garment completed in the **CREATE** stages of the design process. The student has used smooth and highly textural surfaces through knit to create a dynamic garment for menswear.

Interview
Fioen Van Balgooi

Fioen van Balgooi studied fashion and textile design in the Netherlands. She has experience in sustainable textiles and **design for disassembly**, and has helped many designers to incorporate sustainable design practices into their work.

20 Fioen Van Balgooi

Where do your research ideas come from?

Most of the time an idea starts with a design problem that needs to be solved. For me, sustainability is very important. Take, for example, removable prints. Everything is temporary. That is the way we should look at decorating our textiles, too. People change, but their clothes do not change with them. We stop wearing our clothes when we are tired of them, while prints are permanent. What would happen if we had the possibility to replace prints on textiles? In other words, to remove prints and add new ones to make fabrics last. This method would combine short (fashion) cycles with long raw-material cycles. Therefore, I designed the concept of removable prints.

How do you start your research?

I first identify the problem. For example, with removable prints, how are prints on textiles normally made? What kind of materials do you need? How is the process done? What is most commonly used in the industry: silkscreen printing or digital printing? These sorts of questions.

Then I brainstorm on what the ideal situation would be: a print that can be easily removed from the textile. What would be needed to make it happen? Which parts of the normal process need to be altered?

And then I search for solutions to alter those steps. And that is mostly the longest and most difficult part. If you change one part, you might need to change more. For example, I changed the ink, then it was difficult to use a digital printer because the new ink clogged the nozzles. So, I had to find the right printer or make an ink for silkscreen printing, but this process needed a thicker ink and then it was not removable anymore.

Why is research important to your work?

Without research, you do not know if your design really is a solution to a problem. For me, textile design is never solely about the looks, it is about functionality and making products more sustainable. However, looks are very important. Choosing the right colours that appeal to people and make them want to use it cannot be underestimated. Because if people do not like the design they are not going to buy it in the first place, no matter how environmentally friendly your design is.

I look at the textile industry and sometimes I get irritated by the way things are currently done and I want to change them, like with the removable prints.

Can you tell me about your design process? How do you generate ideas?

I sit down with a piece of paper and make a mindmap. I write down and draw all ideas that come to mind and connect the ones that relate with lines. I brainstorm on different words that have to do with the subject. And from all those disorderly doodles I get some ideas that I give a try. Then I make some first sketches of how it might look and work out the ones that seem promising.

21 Fioen experiments with a range of processes to create beautifully crafted textile creations.

Where and who have you worked with/for?

Since 2009 I have worked for more than eighty customers as a freelance design consultant. Most customers are designers or people from research and development departments who I helped with sourcing sustainable materials or brainstorming during the design process on how to change the design so it can, for example, be reused, recycled or create less waste. I have been to material fairs in France, Italy and Germany to search for new sustainable materials and talk to suppliers.

Since 2015 I have worked for MVO Nederland (CSR Netherlands) as a knowledge manager, where I have worked on some textile projects, mainly focused on distributing knowledge about sustainable textiles to Dutch brands and creating collaborations. My focus in this job is less on designing textiles or products and more on facilitating companies in the process of becoming sustainable. This could mean contributing to a brainstorming session, bringing companies from the supply chain together or doing desk research on a specific topic.

Who or what has had the most influence on your work?

Years ago, when I was studying at the Art Academy, I came across the concept of cradle to cradle (from Michael Braungart and William McDonough) and immediately became inspired. For me this meant I could make beautiful things, as many designers want, but without harming the

22 Testing and sampling is an essential part of the textile design process. Colour, permanence of dye and handle must be tested before final samples are made.

environment. The concept for me changed my view of environmentally friendly designing, from a guilt feeling (we need to use and do as little as possible) towards an abundance of possibilities (if we design things in such a way we can reuse the materials, then we do not create waste any more). I did my Master's research on 'How can a fashion designer create a different mindset in order to design eco-effectively?', which was based on the concept of cradle to cradle. After graduating I followed the cradle-to-cradle design course from EPEA and then I started my freelance design consultancy work. Now the concept of cradle to cradle is part of the broader concept of the **circular economy**, of which you find a lot of information through the Ellen MacArthur foundation.

23 Fioen uses print to let her audience know that her designs are aiming to be more environmentally sustainable.

24 Fioen has created a textural/weathered cloth that appears to have a leather like contemporary appeal.

What do you feel is the greatest achievement to date?

I want to help as many designers as possible with my inspiration, advice and network so they can make products from good materials that can be easily recycled or biodegraded. In one of my projects I helped a company in their search for biodegradable materials for insoles. We first identified the functionalities (e.g. moisture wicking, dimensionally stable, tear resistant, made from natural materials), then I went to a material fair in Italy and spoke to many different suppliers. In the end the insoles where made with some of my suggestions and they have been sold in large retail stores in the Netherlands in almost every city. All those people who are now walking on those insoles are walking on much more environment-friendly insoles thanks to my help.

25 Explorative sculptural pieces that cross the boundaries between textiles and jewellery design.

Do you have any advice for those thinking of a career in textile design?
Make it matter! What would you like to add to this world? Make that with respect for the environment and all living creatures in it. Do not create waste. Search for biodegradable and recyclable fibres, keep design for disassembly in mind while making products from the textiles. And innovate; maybe you are the one who uses fibres that filter pollutants from the air while being worn as a textile.

For inspiration, take a look at www.refinity.eu

26 The natural environment is key to all of Fioen's work and she blends imagery, print processes and photography here to highlight why we need to be constantly attentive to how we design.

Case Study

Freddie Robins

Freddie Robins' work crosses definable categories of craft, art and design. She uses what is traditionally seen as a craft medium (wool) and craft skills (knitting) to express concepts, which are more usually expressed through fine art mediums. Freddie also uses automated industrial knitting machinery that is usually employed by commercial designers. Knitting is her preferred textile method to explore pertinent contemporary issues of gender and the human condition, as she finds knitting to be a powerful medium for self-expression and communication because of the cultural preconceptions surrounding it. Her work subverts these preconceptions and disrupts the notion of the medium being passive and benign. Her ideas are often expressed through an exploration of the human form. These works question physical normality, incorporating humour and fear, a reoccurring theme in Freddie's work. The titles are integral to the work: a play on words to enhance the material objects.

27 *Someone else's dream,* 2014–2016
Series of re-worked hand knitted jumpers, mixed fibres. Installed at Forty Hall, Enfield, North London.

28 *Bad Mother*, 2013
Machine-knitted wool, machine-knitted Lurex, expanding foam, knitting needles, glass beads, sequins, dress pins, crystal beads on maple wood shelf, 780 × 160 × 160 mm.

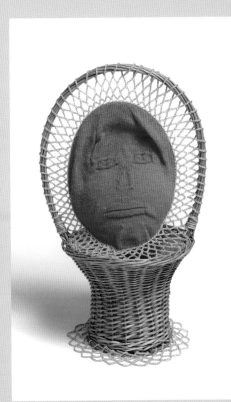

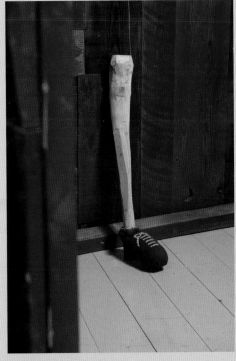

30 *... dances like*, 2017
Machine- and hand-knitted wool, wadding, cherry wood. Installed at The Minories Art Gallery, Colchester.
All photographs by Douglas Atfield

29 *Basketcase*, 2015
Machine-knitted wool, crocheted Lurex, wicker basket, 260 × 520 × 260 mm.

Case Study

Yinka Shonibare

Yinka Shonibare is a British-Nigerian contemporary artist, currently working in London. Much of his work explores colonialism and post-colonialism through painting, sculpture, photography, film and performance. He frequently uses textiles in his creations, often to symbolize cultural,

racial and sociological meaning. His work has been exhibited worldwide, including at the Brooklyn Museum, New York, The Museum of African Art at the Smithsonian Institution, Washington DC, and on the fourth plinth at Trafalgar Square in London.

31 The installation 'Scramble for Africa' by British artist of Nigerian origin Yinka Shonibare is pictured during a press preview of the exhibition 'Who Knows Tomorrow' on 2 June 2010 at the Friedrichswerdersche Kirche in Berlin.

To paint A2 versions of these?

Composition

The Textile Design Process

In this chapter we will begin exploring the textile design process with how to find information. Where should your idea start?

It is usually best to start with you! What information is directly available to you within your own environment, your everyday life and in your cultural and personal background? We all have different points of visual reference, either from our travels, our homes, our history or places we like to visit. All of these day-to-day experiences contain a rich source of visual information, which we can put to good use and generate ideas regarding a context. It is therefore important to consider how these 'close to home' references might be a starting point for your project.

Consider next how you might gain access to certain sites of information? Public buildings, for example museums, galleries and railway stations, are all easily accessible and contain both **primary** and **secondary sources** (which will be explained in detail). Who do you know who can perhaps provide you with additional access and information? Consider contacting organizations or companies that might be of interest and able to help you with your research. In essence, the textile design process is about research and methods for undertaking research and generating ideas.

32 Student sketchbook page showing the original photograph of materials found on a street. Being visually attentive to what is on your doorstep and training your eye to 'look and see' is an important part of being a designer.

> **Research is first – if you're not interested, you never can find something.**
> Issey Miyake

Exploring the IDEA through Textile Research Methods

What is Contextual Research?

Designers are primarily concerned with designing for people. Therefore, contextual research investigates who you are designing for, as understanding the context or the likely end user is paramount to ensure that your design work is highly relevant. Sometimes this information can be set within the brief, or you might be asked to identify a particular context yourself.

What is Primary Visual Research?

Primary visual research refers to objects, places or situations that you find and experience yourself, something that you see, hear or touch, for example. As a textile designer, this information might be found on a research trip where you record what you are seeing and experiencing through drawing, painting, mark making or photography. As well as the destination, the journey itself may become part of your research. Primary visual research is a direct type of research that involves all your senses in response to your surroundings.

Therefore, primary visual research is the essential ingredient for all textile design research and complements your knowledge and understanding of textile contexts, since you should have an awareness of what you are collecting visual information for.

33 Student sketchbook pages. It is important to look at and analyse what surrounds you in the world of art and design and beyond. This student was researching the Bauhaus movement (Germany 1919–1933), and you can see their interest in the iconic graphics from this era.

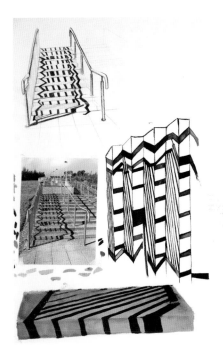

34 These student sketchbook pages show how a photograph of shadows on a stair was used as the primary research to explore various pattern structures. The student uses the sketchbook as a worksheet to try out various pattern options.

I trawl flea markets, car boot sales and vintage boutiques for amazing items. That's where I look for vintage textiles, old embroideries and pieces of haberdashery, as well as things that have incredible colours, fantastic textures and interesting histories. I decorate the studio with it all, and it transforms my studio into one big mood board.

Karen Nicol

What is Primary Contextual Research?

Primary contextual research requires you to look, think and explore the world of textiles through experiencing textiles themselves. This includes handling cloth, using cloth, observing how others use cloth or the role cloth has within different cultures. By doing this you will build up knowledge and an understanding of cloth; how it acts, drapes, moves and how people respond to it and live with it. It may involve having conversations or interviews with other people, listening to someone tell a story, or may relate to something that you have had experience of yourself.

Getting out and about is a very important part of being a designer. It is necessary for primary research collection, but is also crucial to help you find out what others are doing first hand. It is good to visit places where people make or sell textiles. Shops that specialize in vintage and contemporary textiles are a joy to visit for any textile designer as they house design products that range from clothing to blankets. Keep an eye on what is out there via the internet as designers' websites contain many products and prices for you to see. It is also a good idea to visit places where people make and sell their own work, such as artists' studios, craft fairs and open days where you can talk to practitioners themselves.

Quite simply, primary research (both visual and contextual) impacts on all stages of the design process, as it is the stimulus and quality of primary research that makes the designer want to design and express their personal language.

Author Tip

Make sure that you have a good collection of drawing materials with you. It is a good idea to make a portable toolkit using a small toolbox that has a range of different media and papers. Also have a small sketchbook with you to quickly make sketches, write down notes and ideas and to collect things that might interest you.

35a There are plenty of places to visit to look at textiles, some may be on your doorstep, or they may be further afield. Markets take place in every corner of the globe and often sell textiles from different places around the world.

35b Shops that sell textiles or fashion and homewares products are good to explore. These can be commercial high-street outlets or more specialized boutiques.

36 Collecting tools that suit how you want to work is very important. However, it is good to relate what type of medium and tools you use to your drawing source. In other words, choose a medium and tools that will convey the essence of your source.

Exercise – Textile Observation

Think of yourself as an explorer observing something for the first time. Look in places that are familiar to you but where you might not have looked previously. When you stop and take time to observe, you will begin to see subtle changes in colour on what appears to be a white wall, or a variation in form on each leaf on that tree or a **pattern** emerging through the sunlit shadows of venetian blinds.

It is a textile designer's ability to seek out design potential from everyday surroundings that makes them special.

37 Secondary research is invaluable when seeking information that you may not be able to access first hand. These microscopic images of snowflakes capture form, texture, colour and pattern. All very important ingredients for the textile designer.

Author Tip

When you are out on location, try and record as much information as possible. You may not be able to re-visit and it is important that you have enough information to start developing your design drawings.

What is Secondary Research?

Secondary research is different from primary research in that you do not experience a phenomenon yourself, but instead see it through the eyes of someone else. This applies to both visual and contextual research. Secondary research is crucial to help deepen and expand your knowledge of textiles and textile design. You can use books, the internet, TV documentaries, films, news or political debate to find out more about any subject.

Secondary research is often gathered from sources such as books, films, magazines and digital sources. It is invaluable, especially if you want to see something that is hard to find yourself, for example, snow crystals through a microscope. Secondary research is also critical to help you to understand historical and contemporary concepts such as **Bauhaus** or Japanese textiles and to help you to understand the different contexts for textile design. However, it is important to balance both primary and secondary sources in order to be well informed and innovative.

Secondary research also enables you to find out about new materials and to discover what other new developments are happening within the textiles arena. Through secondary research, you discover things about your subject on a global scale and this helps to build your own knowledge base. Therefore, secondary research is just as important as primary research and you should endeavour to balance both.

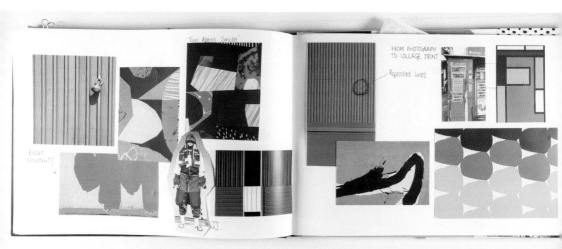

38 This student is using industrial type doors and street furniture to inspire their work, looking at the colour, shapes, patterns and textures from which to pull information.

Where to Find Ideas

Look at anything that is of interest or importance to you and fits with your idea.

Our environments vary across cultures and over time. This is what makes each designer different, as plants and natural forms, colours and light, architectural forms and materials and so on vary in every part of the world.

Galleries and museums provide us with knowledge about the history of a culture as well as cultural artefacts. As a textile researcher you can develop your own ideas from researching cultural artefacts. It is helpful to look at some of the techniques used by other cultures in pattern, structure and **composition**, but it is all about looking and synthesizing what you are researching, so that you can use it in your own way.

Inspiration is usually very indirect; it can take lots of different shapes and forms which can also be influenced by timing. To name but a few: Dutch design, Josef Frank, William Morris, Joseph Beuys, Paul Klee, Leonardo, Picasso, Ridley Scott, Tom Kirk, Chuck Mitchell, Italian motorcycles, Jake and Dinos Chapman, Ricky Gervais, Mona Hatoum and so on.
Timorous Beasties

Exercise – Drawing 1

Visit a historical collection in a museum or an art gallery. It could also be a historic building such as a stately home with a personal collection of historic and/or antique artefacts. Take with you a sketchbook and some dry media, for example, pens and pencils. A small watercolour box with a container or jar for water might be allowed. Make sure that you ask permission first, as they often have guidelines on materials that you can bring with you and use. If you want to take photographs, seek permission first as many collections do not allow the use of photography.

Select an object that you find interesting. It can be a textile, a piece of clothing, jewellery, a ceramic, perhaps even a piece of furniture. Any object or collection that you are drawn to. What are the different qualities you can see in terms of colour, surface and so on? Look for interesting patterns and shapes; look at the colours, have they faded through time or use? Look at the surface quality. Try and capture the qualities in your sketching. Do not try and resolve drawings but rather try and capture the 'essence' of what you are looking at in study drawings. You will need to make a number of drawings using different techniques here. Consider taking a 'line for a walk' by drawing the outline of the object in one continuous line where your pen or paper remains on the page. Try and illustrate the textural qualities and pattern. By doing these studies you can then take them away to analyse and develop further. Always make sure you have captured enough information as it is not always possible to revisit. Do not rely on photographs or digital reproductions, nothing can inform you better than through actually visiting, seeing and analysing. This will enable you to develop your own unique interpretation.

Galleries tend to focus on contemporary artefacts and practices, although many have a permanent collection that exemplifies art and design from a historical perspective. Galleries vary what they show and many focus on fine art, which includes paintings, sculptures, conceptual pieces, films, videos, photography and installations. Some galleries focus on design, such as the Design Museum in London, or the Cooper Hewitt National Design Museum in New York, and others show contemporary craft. Look up galleries in your area and find some that show contemporary products for you to visit. Going to see current exhibitions is a great way of keeping up to date with what is going on and meeting people!

39 The V&A Museum, Dundee, Scotland, designed by Kengo Kuma. Museums like the V&A hold many cultural artefacts to research. Students are usually very welcome when they seek permission to sit and draw within museums, just ask!

Photography

Photography is an excellent way to gather primary information, but you must think about how you use your camera or phone. The camera is your research tool, so consideration needs to be given to how it is used and what it is used for. Remember that you are searching for and recording imagery through the lens to develop further. Think carefully about what you compose in the frame. Make decisions about composition and how light and colour are balanced. Are you close enough to see the textures or surfaces that you need for your research? Have you captured and composed the structures that will be of use to you? The camera provides a different type of visual research; it has its own qualities that can be exploited fully in the development process through digital software packages such as Photoshop and Illustrator.

Digital Tools

Software packages such as Adobe Creative Suite contain a multitude of digital tools that are increasingly utilized by artists and designers in conjunction with hand processes. Developing your skills, particularly within Photoshop and Illustrator, enable you to rapidly develop your visual ideas, which can then be analysed and selected for further development.

40 This student drawing shows how they have collaged their own photographs into their drawing, giving the overall image greater depth. Think of innovative ways to use your photographs beyond 'copying' them. Think about how you can translate or incorporate your own photographs into your work.

> A photograph is not only an image (as a painting is an image), an interpretation of the real; it is also a trace, something directly stencilled off the real, like a footprint or a death mask.
> Susan Sontag

> Even when I work with computers, with high technology, I always try to put in the touch of the hand.
> Issey Miyake

Periodicals

Periodicals refer to scholarly publications that are produced at regular intervals and can be a useful reference. Within textile design, this would normally be a journal, which contains a collection of written pieces that are up to date and current. Academic publications and journals contain subject-specific information written and reviewed by experts in their field.

These publications will give you varied types of information regarding a whole range of issues relating to design. This might include gender and historical debates and the politics of work, craft methods or current research practices. They are important publications that inform the audience about contemporary practices within the wider area of design. Crucially, they are a key means by which information based on scholarly research is shared throughout the field. College and university libraries can help you access journals that relate to the subjects being taught.

Magazines

Magazines are an excellent way to access popular topics that relate to your subject area and there is an abundance of them to choose from. They vary in the type of information they contain and many of them focus on fashion or interior textile products. Some specialist textile publications devote the entire publication to textiles and textile issues. Fashion-forecasting magazines are helpful as they contain information regarding forecasting trends that are used within the textiles industry.

There are many popular magazines that have visual information (photography) of fashion and interior design, and feature articles regarding various popular topics. It is worth browsing more mainstream fashion and interiors magazines, as they are excellent snapshots of contemporary popular culture.

There are also fantastic technology magazines full of all the latest information on new materials and fabrics. These centre on material investigation and innovation in textiles. Such information can help you to understand the breadth of the area that you are working within and become quite important as you become more experienced.

Using the Internet

The internet is by far the most accessible method for finding and gathering information today. Through the use of search engines, we can immediately find an enormous number of linked websites and sources for researching any subject worldwide. The internet is a vital tool for finding information quickly and providing us with up-to date design trends and commentary. It is, however, important not to rely solely on internet research for projects. It is fantastic for putting us in touch with companies and specialist information. However, internet research should never be used alone. Other types of research need to be used in conjunction with these methods to keep us in touch with other considerations: the tactile quality of materials and 3D forms and patterns, for example.

Digital Platforms

There is now an abundance of online sources to browse through, allowing access to contemporary design and designers. Platforms like Instagram are a good source for visual references and also an ideal site to archive your digital material. YouTube is also a great resource to find filmed footage on a vast range of topics, from TED talks to 'how to' information relating to designing and making.

Books

For textile design, there is a wealth of books available. Textbooks are useful to learn new processes, as they help to direct practical knowledge. Also, books about well-known designers and design movements such as Bauhaus, theoretical books, historical textiles and cultures can help to increase your knowledge around design as a subject. Essentially, books help you to further your own practice and help you to think about and analyse subjects. This ultimately helps you to understand textile design within many different contexts.

Historical Archives

As a textile designer, it is important that you develop a good understanding of the rich heritage of textiles. By researching previous textile designs from over the centuries, we are able to understand how and why certain fabrics were created and to question their relevance to design today and for the future.

For textiles, historical research can come from many different sources, some directly related to textiles, for example through fashion, interiors and furnishing, and through other design subjects such as ceramics, jewellery and costume. Large galleries and museums are often wonderful places to find a vast selection of decorative arts in one place. But there are also many smaller collections available in other national and regional galleries and museums. Often, appointments can be made with the collection's curator to view certain periods or types of artefacts from the museum or gallery archive, which are not on public display.

41 Crazy pattern quilting was a very popular American textiles patchwork technique in the late nineteenth century. The patches and borders were designed using an eclectic mix of patterns.

Using the Library

The library is often the best place to start exploring a research project as you have instant access to a wide range of reference material, both text and image-based. After brainstorming you will have some idea about where to start looking. When visiting the library, try to be open-minded and allow plenty of time to explore different sections and book aisles on subjects that might at first seem unrelated to your project. Unlike the internet, using a book is a completely different type of experience, being both visually stimulating and physically inspiring through the physical touch and smell that is offers. It is important to remember that books in themselves are beautifully crafted objects. Looking at the layout of contemporary and original, historical manuscripts can provide far more enriching sources of inspiration than are likely to be found on any website page.

Visual Research

Visual research involves looking at things closely. This may sound easy, but it is much harder than you think; it relies on your being open to what you see in a whole sense, and allowing yourself to relax and respond to visual stimuli. It is about recording and documenting information that can be processed through the IDEA and DEVELOP stage. It relies on you thinking deeply about what you are seeing, and capturing the essence of the environment in your drawing or photographs.

42 **Student sketch showing investigation of colour, structure, texture, form and composition. The student conveys the chaos of the building site source extremely well through their mixed-media approach.**

Visual research is crucial to every designer and it is important to learn to be curious about what you are looking at so that there is a continuous driving passion for design development.

> **I can study an insect forever, noticing the gossamer textures of their wings and the soft fibres that cover their shells.**
> Kahori Maki

Observation Techniques

Always try to remember that you are gathering information that you can use in the DEVELOP stage. You are not necessarily drawing 'a picture' in the traditional sense. It is important to think of your research as 'information gathering' at all times, as it is the first and most crucial stage of your idea process.

It may help to consider your page as a study sheet where you can record forms, shapes, interesting surfaces, patterns or colours in detail. You may also have to try and think differently about how you are looking. Try zooming in to see close up, or try looking at something via a mirror just to see it in a different way. Look at things from different angles or take photographs and then examine them. Use your imagination at this stage in order to see potential in the everyday.

Drawing

Drawing for textile design is often misunderstood. Many see it as a chore that must be completed before the 'real' work of design can begin. Drawing, however, is fundamental to the design process and instrumental in providing a rich source of material on which a design can be based. Traditional techniques for drawing are not always the most relevant and you should develop your own individual style of drawing to create your own personal signature.

There is no 'right' way to draw. Some people are very good at observational or 'realistic' drawing, where their understanding of proportion, scale and composition provides a very accurate representation of their subject. This does not, however, necessarily mean that they are good textile designers. Drawing is essentially about ideas, testing things out, experimenting and trying to visualize from a wide range of approaches. Drawing is a dynamic and highly creative process and ultimately the backbone to all of your design work.

43 Student drawing using collage and oil pastel. Changing the colour of the paper you work on can have a dramatic impact on the final piece. In this work the vibrancy of the oil pastels works well on red paper to convey the energy of the source.

Tools and Methods for Unpacking the Idea

In this section we will look at the toolkit for idea generation to enable a deeper understanding of different approaches to research. Research for textiles should include materials and visualization processes at every stage of production, and it is vital that there is a holistic design approach between context, materials and visuals throughout.

The Sketchbook

The sketchbook is the most important tool that you have. They come in many different shapes and sizes from small A5 (148 × 210 mm) to larger A2 (594 × 420 mm). They can be bound hardbacks, spiral-bound or loosely bound at the top to enable pages to be taken out. You should decide which is the best size to use depending on how you intend to use it. For example, do you want to carry it with you at all times to record your thoughts as well as your observations? If so, an A2 might be too large. Do you want the pages to come out? If so, the bound hardbacks will not be suitable. Before you buy, think about how you will use it and buy one to suit you and the way that you work.

Think of the sketchbook as your creative companion. Record primary visual information and write your ideas and observations down. Include information on artists and designers you feel inspired by. This can be postcards from exhibitions, information on colour and contextual resources. The sketchbook is a reflective tool that allows you to go back and forward through your research and development in a continuous way.

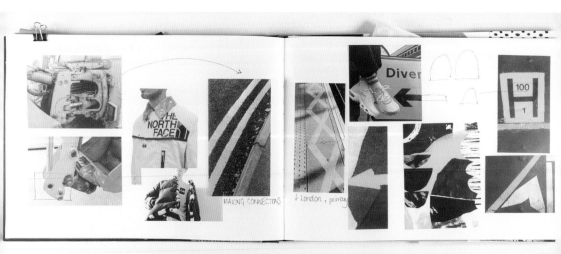

44 This student sketchbook shows the links between contextual and visual research. The student's own photography of machinery and road markings are linked with signage and outerwear to create a dynamic mood.

Drawing Materials

Before you start to draw, it is vital that you choose appropriate materials to draw with that empathize with the visual source. Essentially, this means that you must think about the source and materials as one, and choose materials that will work to translate this. It is helpful to think about your source in the following way: is the source fragile, solid, transparent, opaque, rich and colourful? Then choose materials that will be sympathetic to the feel or mood of the subject. Take time to think about what you are looking at and always analyse the qualities of the subject that you are drawing in order to select an appropriate medium to draw with.

Primary Materials For Drawing

Pencils: 8B, 6B, 4B, 2B, HB

Small pencil sharpener

Charcoal pencils: 6B, 2B, white

Compressed charcoal: several sticks

Vine charcoal: soft, several sticks

Rubbers: kneaded and vinyl

Pastels: wax crayons

Gouache

Watercolours

India ink: black and assorted colours

Drawing ink: sepia or burnt umber

Penholder and nibs (one must have a point for drawing)

Several bristled brushes: large and small

Fixative (optional)

Masking tape

Fingers!

Techniques to Explore within your Drawing

Wash and Ink

Wash and ink is a very simple technique. It creates a range of spontaneous marks, strokes and lines made by ink or pens that essentially 'bleed' with the wet surface.

Firstly, wet your paper surface with water. You can use a sponge for this, or paint it on with a large brush. Next, using a pen tip dipped in ink, or similar (maybe even a stick or a feather), start to draw onto the washed paper. The line of the ink will immediately start to run. Experiment with this technique and find ways to control the effect. You can do this in a number of ways. Change the type of paper surface – what happens if you use a watercolour paper compared with cartridge paper? Try saturating the paper in different degrees to control the bleeding. Also experiment with having some areas of the paper washed and others not.

You can also use wash techniques such as 'discharge', where the colour is taken out by the 'wash'. Try painting over with ink and then drawing with bleach.

There is something magical in seeing what you can do, what texture and tone and colour you can produce merely with a pen point and a bottle of ink.
Ida Rentoul Outhwaite

45 Student sketchbook pages showing observation drawing using wash and ink. The use of black ink onto white paper conveys a sense of power in the image.

Using Paint and Pencil

You will be familiar with using some types of paint. Gouache and watercolours are commonly used by designers as they are quick to dry, easy to mix and retain great colour. Working with more than one type of media at the same time, however, requires a slightly different approach – both need to work with and complement each other. Try drawing your subject with a pencil line first. Using a wash of paint, you will see the pencil line coming through under the surface. Next, experiment with using both pencil line and paint to describe your composition.

Sponging and Scratching

Sponging is a technique used for applying paint using a sponge. Large uneven surfaces can be covered and exciting effects can be created. Try using a white wall emulsion paint, which is relatively inexpensive, with a sponge. Once the surface has dried or a crust has formed over the paint surface, you can start to 'scratch' into the paint's surface. A wide range of tools can be used for this – try using sticks, a scalpel, a pencil or even a pin.

46 These observational drawings were made in a park using paint and pencil. Each quick sketch provided information that can be developed further back in the studio.

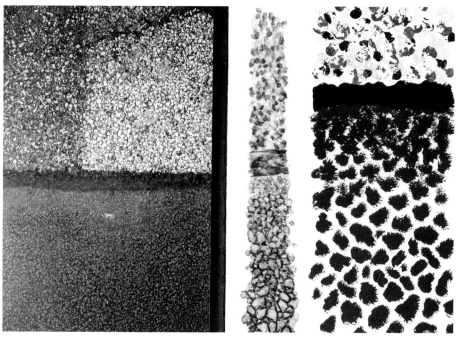

47 Example of student work which shows the translation of photographing imagery through sponging techniques to create a surface that can be further developed through materials.

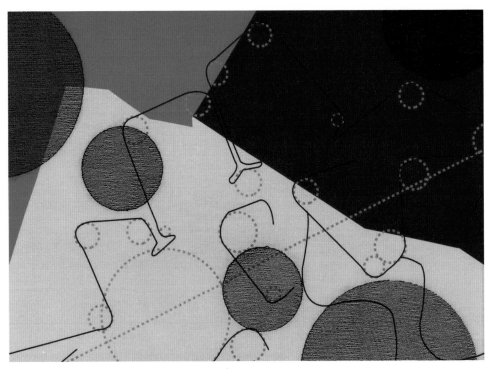

48a This student work is an example of digital embroidery and print and shows how stitch can be used as a drawing tool.

Drawing with Stitch

A sewing machine can also be used as a drawing tool. By removing the sewing foot, you can begin to 'free-stitch' to create unusual lines. Try using the sewing machine without any thread. Hold your paper up to the light to see the effect that the holes have made on the paper.

Making Marks

As previously mentioned, mark making plays an important role in creating dynamic surface effects that can then be translated into textiles. Many of the techniques detailed can be used to create a range of spontaneous marks on paper or other surfaces.

48b Student drawing with stitch.

Exercise – Drawing 2

First, select some objects to observe. Rather than trying to anticipate what your drawing may look like using particular objects, try to choose objects that have some meaning or narrative. Arrange these objects close together, perhaps on their side, upside down or on top of each other. Next make a viewer by cutting out a 4 × 4 cm (1.5 × 1.5 in.) window from the centre of an A4 (A (letter)) sheet of paper. Start to move your window around your objects, looking for an interesting composition.

Using large sheets of paper, preferably A1 (D), you are now ready to create a series of quick, dynamic drawings, each time using a different media. These might include:

- permanent marker
- pencil
- graphite stick
- biro
- fine liner
- large brush
- wax crayon, or
- charcoal.

Try to stand while drawing as this will increase your range of movement and arm extension. Work on the drawing exercises directly over the top of one another using the same piece of paper. Change your viewfinder position and rotate your paper between each exercise.

Drawing from Memory
Look carefully at your objects for two minutes – try and capture in your mind the shapes of the objects together in your composition viewfinder. Cover up the objects and now draw from your memory.

Continuous Line Drawing
Draw your subject, keeping your eyes on the subject matter the whole time. You must keep your pen in contact with the paper without looking at your drawing. Time yourself for two minutes.

Tape Drawing
Draw your composition with a double line of masking tape only. Again, make every line work for you and time yourself for two minutes. Try enlarging your work by taping your drawing tool to the end of a long stick. You will need to put your paper on the floor and rearrange the position of your objects – again, limit your time.

Repeat all of these exercises with differing media overlapping on the page. The timed, fast pace of the exercise should help you to observe quickly and produce fast and dynamic drawing. It is vital that you review the drawings you have made. Using masking tape, paper windows or your camera, identify areas of interest. This might be the varying quality of marks, the composition or the new structures that have been made.

Remember that this is all part of the drawing process. You should now have sheets of interesting surfaces and marks. You may see a sense of energy in the mark making or possibly a sensitivity that is a reflection of your chosen subject matter. In a relatively short space of time you have generated a vast amount of work – you have evaluated it and selected areas to progress with that can then relate to textile techniques to help you translate these drawings into textiles.

The boundaries between design disciplines are becoming increasingly blurred. We see textile designers today working with many other types of materials. This offers new exciting possibilities and observational drawing techniques using mixed media are particularly useful in triggering new approaches to textiles.

Mixed media refers to the process of combining two or more types of media to create a single composition. This technique for observational drawing enables many different surfaces and textures to be made. Found objects can be used in combination with traditional drawing media, such as paints and pencils.

Mixed media extends the experience of drawing through the use of line, tone, texture, shape and form, using traditional materials together with other types of media such as collage, paint, paper structures and wire, investigating composition in two dimensions and in relief.

Some commonly used mixed-media techniques are outlined here.

Collage

Collage is a technique used for assembling different types of materials together. A collage can include all sorts of materials, such as newspaper and magazine clippings, coloured and handmade papers, photographs, postcards and many other found objects.

49 Example of mixed media by a student. This student has used a combination of paint, inks, felt-tip pens and coloured matchsticks to create marks in their sketches that give a 3D mood.

50 Student sketchbook page showing a bold use of collage to convey the scaffolded structure. The student has used old student union posters to recycle into her work. Collage can be a very powerful way to convey information, particularly if you use interesting papers in the work. Try making your own papers to create colours and marks to collage with.

Relief

Drawing in relief involves building up surfaces. This can be achieved by creating raised areas within a drawing through layering and overlapping collage materials together. Consider using different materials together, by layering tissue paper over another surface, for example, the texture, print or colour will appear through to the outer surface.

Exercise – Collage

Gather together a range of found paper-based materials. These might include used envelopes and stamps, cardboard, old dress patterns, maps, newspaper, bus tickets or shopping receipts. Using an A2 (C) sheet of paper, begin to assemble and glue your found objects whilst at the same time observing your composition (as for drawing techniques). Consider the shapes and forms of the objects and how they overlap. Rip, shred and cut paper edges to reflect the composition. This collage can then be further developed using traditional drawing materials to add detail and colour.

51 Student drawing using various weights of paper, paint, ink and stencil cutting to create an additional surface and provide contrast. Note the interesting layering through stencil cutting the page to reveal the marks on the next sheet.

Observing Lines

Investigating line within your composition can be done in a number of ways that do not always involve 'drawing' on a flat surface. Drawing using a sewing machine is one way of doing this. Wire can also be used to investigate the 3D space. To do this, choose a pliable wire that can be easily bent and twisted.

Try also cutting into paper with a scalpel to create repetitive and patterned lines. This technique changes the handle and quality of the paper where it will begin to 'sag' or bend to create different relief effects.

AUTHOR TIP

Here are some ways to alter the quality of your paper:

- folding
- bending
- rolling
- twisting
- tearing
- crumpling
- cutting
- shredding
- puncturing
- scoring
- weaving
- layering
- slotting
- mushing.

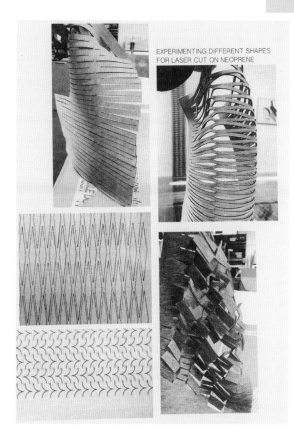

EXPERIMENTING DIFFERENT SHAPES FOR LASER CUT ON NEOPRENE

52 Student piece using open cut work through laser cutting to create line patterns. Cutting into the fabric causes the form to change from a simple surface line to a 3D structure on the body.

Exercise – Scale-Drawing

Using an existing drawing, mark out a 10 × 10 cm area masking or covering the rest of the picture. Using just monotone, redraw this area at a scale of 25 × 25 cm and also 4 × 4 cm.

Scale can be used to investigate a subject from different perspectives. As mentioned previously, drawing for textile design is primarily concerned with investigating detail. This can be done through the surface, the pattern, the texture or the structure.

By zooming in on an area, you can examine the minutiae, as a scientist would do, of the subject. You may, however, want to observe and record this on a completely different scale. You can do this in a number of ways.

First, you can draw what we are seeing to a larger or smaller scale. You can also use different tools such as photocopying or projecting an image. By drawing or photocopying onto acetate, you can use an overhead projector to project onto a wall. Using large sheets of paper taped to the wall, you can then redraw to a completely new scale. Smaller scale is also possible and is used a lot for putting drawn images into a **repeat** pattern. It is also possible to reduce or enlarge the detail of drawings through photocopying or scanning onto the computer.

2D Drawing

2D drawing refers to a drawing technique whereby only the length and width dimensions are shown. In observational drawing, we are literally 'flattening' a composition, removing any additional information that provides depth and illusion. This can be a very useful technique for design drawing. Drawing from a bird's-eye viewpoint is a good example of how to put this into practice. By observing your composition from a position directly above, you will notice how the relationship between objects changes. Any shadowing or reflection can be observed as flat.

3D Drawing

3D drawing adds the further dimension of depth. This is where perspective, working with light and shade in drawing, adds a 3D quality. Drawing can also be done in three dimensions – paper or a different surface can be cut or manipulated into 3D forms. Describing your subject as a 3D form enables you to consider your composition from a new perspective.

3D into 2D

A useful method for exploring drawing is to transfer from one dimension to another. Using a single sheet of paper, cut, fold and stick it to reshape it into a 3D form. This is now your object for 2D drawing. Using another sheet of the same paper, draw your 3D form in monotone using just line.

53 Student work looking closely at insect forms. The 3D structures of these animals are inspirational as the student looks for and collects other contextual information relating to the textures, forms and marks they see.

54 Cutting and reforming paper can be an inspiring source from which to create drawings. Experiment with different papers to see how they hold their shape. Japanese artist Yuken Teruya uses brown paper shopping bags to create exquisite hand-cut miniature trees.

Textile designers frequently collect things that they see and touch. They often collect their sources in order to refer back to them as they work. This achieves three things: it provides them with a visual source with which they can examine colour and texture, and so on. It also provides them with something they can physically hold (it may be the coolness, roughness, smoothness or weight of the 'source' that inspired them). And having the source to hand (which may be an object) helps to relive experiences. This is important, as it is the **sensory** experiences that can influence the designer in how they begin to translate and develop their ideas.

55 Mind mapping is an excellent way to get all your thoughts out on paper and make connections between all your ideas. You can work on this digitally or simply create hand-drawn maps that you can add to in a physical way.

Brainstorming and Mind-Mapping Techniques

The term 'brainstorming' is commonly used to describe methods for generating initial ideas quickly. Group sessions are very helpful in this situation, but brainstorming can also be effective when done on your own. In group situations, ideas and thoughts can be shared to help broaden areas of thinking. Usually, one person from the group will be responsible for writing down all the words using Post-it Notes to explore ideas. A word or an image is enough, rather than a long description. When all possible thoughts have been investigated, the list of words is often extensive. Now you can begin to re-examine this list again. Decide on the words that are the most important. Highlight keywords and towards the end of the brainstorming session put these into a list of priority. The work generated

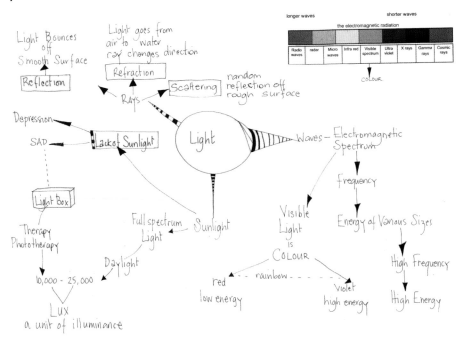

from this session can now be used as a reference point both at the start and throughout the life of your project.

Brainstorming is one way in which to generate ideas. Another method commonly used for brainstorming is mind mapping. Mind maps are visual maps of ideas. Starting with a central idea they span out from this, usually in a circular shape. As you draw branches from your central idea, you add on keywords, colours and images. They are an excellent tool as they can help you to visualize your thinking, by breaking down your thoughts into the most important keywords – making it easier to make connections and associations.

Theme

Words and images may be used as the creative catalyst for starting your research project. The advantage of this approach is the manner in which you can personalize the project by providing a unique creative perspective. They can be used to express your own individuality, your viewpoints and interests. It is important to remember that good designers bring their own narrative to design, which is vital for creating your own **visual language**.

When considering a theme, you need to select a starting point that will stimulate you creatively. This will need to be considered in relation to the idea. Often, themes can be developed from a word or an image. As a catalyst, they can then be used as a creative springboard for brainstorming.

Exercise – Exploring The Theme

Select an event that you have experienced over the past year. Consider how you might research this using your own touch, taste, sight, smell and hearing. How might you research this using secondary sources? Where could you visit? Which books could you look at? How might you research this using the internet? What sort of sites do you think might be most helpful?

> Every season I find myself working with new themes, sometimes even ones that oppose each other. For example, Clements Ribeiro once asked for over-the-top designs for a collection they described as 'Frida Kahlo meets Singapore whorehouse', while John Rocha wanted minimal designs that evoked abstract art.
> Karen Nicol

Exercise – Mind-Mapping

Starting in the middle of a blank page, write down or draw the idea that you intend to develop. For this we suggest that you use the page in landscape orientation. Begin to develop related sub-headings around this central theme, connecting each of them to the centre with a line. Using the same process for the sub-headings, generate another layer of lower-level sub-headings connecting each of those to the corresponding sub-theme.

56 These student theme boards show the development of two distinct themes for a textile collection. The student was inspired by the work of others as well as their own drawings.

Mood/Storyboards

A **mood board** or storyboard quite simply captures your gathered visual stimuli – photographs, cuttings, colours, textures, patterns. This might also include examples of fabrics, yarns or accessories. The rule with mood boards is that they must clearly communicate a mood or story. The point of the board is not to formally represent some aspect of the design, but to simply act as inspiration – perhaps providing a starting point for a particular theme or pattern/colour scheme within the DEVELOP phase.

Interview
Karen Nicol

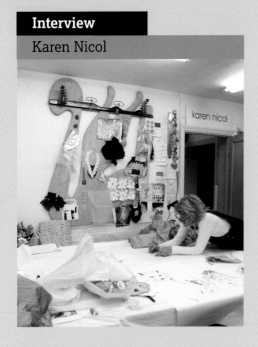

Karen Nicol is an embroidery and mixed-media textile artist working in gallery, fashion and interiors with a London-based design and production studio established for forty years.

57 Karen Nicol working in her studio.

Where do your research ideas come from?

Anywhere and everywhere. I constantly photograph or sketch anything that appeals to me visually, whether it's in a museum or gallery or just the graphics of a slatted gate or the dapple of leaf shadows, an absolutely constant ongoing experience. I don't just look for the project I'm working on at that time but to build an everchanging collection of inspirational images and ideas.

I keep an eye on the media, magazines, film, fashion show websites and so on to try to keep informed of changes in mood and colour.

Flea markets are a big research source where I can find objects and embroideries that are extraordinarily unusual and unique. They are also a wonderful source for materials, which in themselves are enormously inspiring. I have an amazing collection of vintage threads, braids, fabrics, beads, which you could never find in shops.

Working in mixed media I try to keep hyper aware of the qualities and textures of things as well as their visual importance.

How do you start your research?

If I'm answering a brief, everything focuses on the subject matter required. If I'm lucky, ideas start to fill my head of possibilities as soon as I'm told the project and the job is then to refine them and build on them to give them depth, and to try to see a fresh way of handling the idea. Often, working in this business you may only have a day or two at the most to research and sample, which means that you have to act quickly. Years of collecting my personally chosen images and materials have given me a wonderful 'idea' archive, which helps.

Why is research important to your work?

Visual research is incredibly important in my work, it feeds my imagination and ideas and prevents them from getting stale and becoming repetitive. Research energizes one's work in a remarkable way, and when you start to mix different stimuli it changes into something truly personal. I strongly believe that each individual's way of looking at things and their personal taste is their most important asset in designing. Our personal view on things is the only thing that makes us different from all the other amazing designers and artists, so the biggest danger is to narrow your research to just looking at what other people are doing.

It is also so exciting to find that one's reaction to the same visual 'feed' changes as styles in everything around us change.

58 This commissioned quilt was designed to commemorate the 140th anniversary of the iconic Liberty department store in London. Karen takes her inspiration from the shop's Tudor-inspired exterior built using the wood from ships. The nautical theme drives her inspiration, with sea and ship motifs including monkey sailors with tattoos.

Can you tell me about your design process? How do you generate ideas?

I start by drawing, sketching ideas really roughly from my visual research. My drawing is mostly for information as I think you only truly 'see' something when you are drawing it, so it's about shapes and colours and the way things work. Then I almost immediately begin to work on fabric. Working in mixed media, paper and pencil/paint and so on cannot replace the fantastic mix of surfaces and mark making for one's experimentation. One's ground fabric and material choice will make an image totally different each time and the marks you make with stitch cannot be represented by drawn lines on paper, so I find I have to draw and sketch with cloth. My constant message to myself is 'just try it, if it doesn't work I can throw it away and I'll have learned something'.

Where and whom have you worked with/for?

I have worked in fashion and interiors and gallery. Always in a freelance capacity. I have worked for many fashion designers such as Schiaparelli and Alexander McQueen. In interiors I have worked with interior designers and for private clients like the King of Qatar and the Pope, and own-label work for companies like Anthropologie and Designers Guild. Since 2010 I have also worked on art pieces and have had solo shows in London, New York and Paris and exhibited in shows and art fairs all around the world.

59 Karen's fashion collaborations bring her distinctive textile themes and embroidery techniques to the catwalk. This highly embellished garment shows her characteristic 'magpie' approach where she enjoys experimenting with a wide range of different textile methods such as beading, embroidery and fringing.

60 'Ice Bear'. Drawing and sketching is fundamental to Karen's design process. Animals such as this bear are drawn first onto large sheets of tracing paper, then transferred onto fabric and developed using a variety of embellishment techniques and materials. Experimentation is at the heart of her design practice where she is always trying new ideas and never afraid to take risks.

61 'Book Flag'. In this work Karen uses a 'cut and paste' method where she places different textile elements together, similar to a collage page in a sketchbook before finally fixing them in the desired composition. By doing this your ideas can remain fluid and you can explore different layouts before deciding on the final arrangement.

Who or what has had the most influence on your work?

My mother was an embroiderer and painter who became an Ikebana master. I often look at the number of flower designs I do in my work and think how much she taught me. She made my sister and me our own dress blocks when we were thirteen, and we made our own clothes from then, which gave us so much freedom when we weren't concerned about following rules and made me feel I could do anything if I had the courage to try. My tutor Judy Barry at MMU was hugely influential, passing on her total passion for the subject. Other than that there are countless artists who I am in awe of …

62 This embroidered world map incorporates illustrations of natural motifs from across hemispheres to create a highly decorative textile wall piece commissioned for an international bank.

What do you feel is the greatest achievement to date?

I've done some really interesting jobs. I was pretty pleased to get into the Royal Academy summer show, I enjoyed working with Schiaparelli last season. I always tend to hope that what I get to do next will be the best thing I've ever done!

Do you have any advice for those thinking of a career in textile design?

Be passionate and have confidence in your own hand and never miss a deadline.

Case Study

Dries Van Noten

Dries Van Noten is a Belgian fashion designer and formed part of the 'Antwerp Six', a graduate group in the early 1980s from the Royal Academy of Fine Arts of Antwerp who established themselves as a radical fashion collective. Their vision at that time was highly original and unusual. His collections are known for their eclectic and unique prints and patterns, and traditional fabrics, prints and colours from around the world form a distinct part of Van Noten's aesthetic. He is known for his collaborations with textile innovators for creativity and sustainable causes and has been working with artisans and embroiderers in India for many years.

Van Noten has a number of independent stores internationally, including a five-storey former department store in Antwerp. His collections are also sold in over 500 wholesale doors around the world. This is particularly impressive given that the designer does not advertise. He has received many awards and honours for his contribution to fashion including Royal Designer for Industry (RDI), the Gold Medal (Gouden Penning) from the Flemish Chamber of Commerce (VOKA), and the Couture Council Award for Artistry from the Fashion Couture Council of the Museum at FIT in New York.

I'm mad about fabrics and colours.
Dries Van Noten

I try to see that every season we have prints, so that we can work with our six printers. In India we have a cottage industry involving 3,000 people working on many techniques of embroidery, so for me it's important that in every collection we have embroideries. Sometimes they're very in-your-face and visible, sometimes they're subtle. But they're always there, so that I can give work to these people.

63 Detail of Dries Van Noten's work for menswear using embroidery techniques.

64 Dries Van Noten Paris Fashion Week - Menswear F/W 2019–2020.

3

Developing through Material Investigation

This chapter describes in detail how to develop your visual information and will take an in-depth look at the transition between IDEA and CREATE, where material and textile technique and investigation is undertaken. The process is fluid and iterative between IDEA, DEVELOP and CREATE as described in Chapter 1. Ultimately, the DEVELOP stage is the most in depth and requires thorough critical analysis of ideas to translate appropriately through continual reflection and experimentation.

The DEVELOP stage enables you to practise, hone and refine your making skills within textile processes. This is crucial as a textile designer, as 'thinking through making' enables you to understand the possibilities available through idea interpretation and material and process investigation.

There are five key areas that are specific to textiles that we will discuss:

- surface
- texture
- pattern
- structure and
- colour.

65 Student mixed-media textile – wool and cotton with print, embroidery and surface foil decoration.

Colour is fundamental to all areas and will be explained in detail in the next chapter.

What do we Mean by Surface?

Surface in textile design refers in the main to the image, pattern or decorative elements placed on top of the fabric. A surface design can be applied using both flat, 2D techniques such as hand or digital printing, or through a combination of applied techniques, such as mixed media and stitch processes. In order to successfully apply these, all the key areas of pattern, colour, texture and surface must be considered in relation to one another, as it is the combination of these key elements that determines the success of the surface design. Within textile design, the desired outcome is a successful composition that fully integrates the key areas to create innovative surface qualities.

Surface techniques within textiles utilizes traditional technologies such as screen printing and hand stitching and new technologies such as digital printing and digital embroidery. The emergence of new technologies has provided a rich source of process-led investigation that now complements traditional processes. This has opened new possibilities for designers where restrictions of translation through materials are limitless. Students and graduates of textile design courses are now able to position themselves as surface designers, developing new types of practice for those with a background in textile design.

66b This student has used the tweedy surface of cloth to create these abstract textile prints that were inspired by the shapes and surface of cacti. The use of cut paper and collage were used in the development of this work and further enhances the tactile quality of the cloth surface through layering.

66a Inspiration for surface effects can be found all around us. This student drawing is part of a series of studies from the underside of mushrooms. It reminds us that taking time to observe the everyday can bring great creative reward.

Exercise – Surface Effects

Create a 2D surface using scraps of materials such as coloured transparent tissue papers, photographs and recycled materials such as old labels, tickets or wrappers and corrugated paper, to create different surfaces for drawing. Or, using a plain sheet of white paper, choose two or three actions from the following list to create different surface effects:

- layering
- ripping
- scratching
- washing
- creasing
- pleating
- folding
- rubbing
- slashing.

What do we Mean by Texture?

Texture refers to the tactile qualities that can convey a range of 2D/3D surfaces on or integrated within the cloth. Different textures evoke different types of responses and can be used to change the 'form' of the cloth itself. Most textile surfaces invite touch and handling. Texture is synonymous with the feel of the surface of the cloth and also to the illusion of the surface texture. In essence, texture is extremely important to all areas of

> **Textures are a way of representing the union of two feelings: view and touch.**
> Nani Marquina

textile design and should be explored fully within the DEVELOP stage both through sketchbook work and textile materials and processes.

Surface and Texture Techniques

Surface and Texture techniques for sketchbook exploration can include:

COLLAGING. By using a range of different types of materials to create imagery and pattern through collage, a surface can be developed with tactile qualities. You might, for example, sew onto your surface, or scratch into it using sharp tools.

67 Example of student work using a range of processes that can be brought together within the design. These include laser cutting, stitch, print and flocking to create a rich textural 'collage' of surfaces.

Below are some surface and texture techniques for material exploration:

Stamping or Embossing

This is where force or pressure is applied to a surface to create a raised image, motif or decorative element. Often, the force applied can be used to create differences in the surface's thickness.

Printing

Printing techniques are synonymous with creating surface interest. From digital graphic imagery generated through photography to low-tech techniques using hand stencils, sponging and block printing, a base material can be transformed.

Screen Printing

Screen printing can be a playful way to explore how colour and shape can affect the cloth surface. Layering colours and shapes onto the cloth surface can create unexpected details.

Digital Printing

This process has opened up many possibilities as it allows a broader range of marks to be applied to the cloth surface. Combining digital printing with other processes can create innovative fabrics.

68 Sketchbook pages showing how this student uses a technique to create an embossed effect on cloth. The student has used stretch fabrics and vinyl transfers to make the fabric 'pop up'.

69 Digital printing on cloth allows a greater level of flexibility in terms of the range of marks and colours that can be achieved. A textile digital printer is similar to a large-scale paper printer but contains dyes for cloth. Designs for digital printing have to be made on the computer so that they can be printed.

Devoré

This is a process where part of the cloth surface is burned away using a chemical paste. It can be very effective as it can be printed in detail onto the surface of the cloth. It is then 'baked' to facilitate the 'burn out reaction'. It is only successful on a fabric that has a synthetic and natural fibre warp and weft.

Stitch and Mixed Media

There are a vast number of stitch processes that can be used to create surface details on fabric. Hand and machine embroidery are synonymous with textiles across every culture and era. Stitch can be used alone or combined with other processes to enhance the cloth surface. Mixed media includes processes that can build up or cut away a surface to provide textures and patterns.

Developing with Stitch

Machine stitching can be used to develop marks from your original drawings. If you do not have a sewing machine, try stitching paper by hand with a sewing needle. Experiment with pulling the thread to create gathered or ruffled textured areas within your drawing.

70 This student's work illustrates how different surfaces can bring meaning and narrative to textiles. This work uses stitched lines to draw children who have been victims of grief through loss of parents. The depiction of children conveys a poignant sense of emotion through the stitched lines.

Exercise – Mark-Making

Mark-making is a method you can use to create different types of surface interest on paper. These techniques are a great starting point for investigating surface pattern. Using simple drawing tools, often using found objects such as feathers, sticks or sponges, numerous surfaces can be created easily and quickly.

On a large A2 sheet of paper, draw out three rows of 100 × 100 mm squares with a space between each square. Using black and white only, create different surface patterns in each square using a range of found materials. Materials could include all sorts of domestic objects such as sponges, toothbrushes, wire brushes and pastry cutters. Also source natural found objects such as twigs, feathers, fir cones and shells, to name just a few. Using black ink, try and create as many different surface patterns as possible. Experiment with printing, spotting, drawing, flicking, stamping, masking and spraying. Experiment with masking fluid and tape to block areas off. Use resist materials such as wax and crayon. Do not labour over each one, spend only a few minutes on each. At the end of this exercise you should have a sheet with a wide variety of surface patterns. Keep this sheet as a reference point for creating different surfaces to use as part of your drawing material. Write a comment beside each one to remind yourself of the tools and materials you used.

What do we Mean by Pattern?

Pattern is used extensively in textile design, from surface printing to patterns created through the structure of woven and knitted cloth. It is most often used in an aesthetic way; to appeal to the senses, to be beautiful, engaging, soft, comforting, radical or visionary.

Most of us see pattern as a collection of forms, lines, symbols, tones and colours. How you observe and analyse pattern as a textile designer during your initial research stage is fundamental to how the pattern will be developed into a textile design. Pattern is rarely observed in isolation and can be identified, recorded and analysed through the lens of the other key themes identified in this book: colour, surface, structure and texture. Therefore, throughout your research, look for patterns of colour, patterns of structure and patterns within surfaces and textures.

In order to make pattern and become a pattern-maker, you must first begin to recognize it around you within the environment. Understanding and using pattern is an essential part of being a textile designer as it is you, the pattern-maker and designer, who gives pattern its purpose. To fully understand the use of pattern, we will explore the different types of pattern found around us and within textiles. This will enable an understanding of how to find pattern and use it within design.

> In matters of visual form, we sense that nature plays favourites. Among her darlings are spirals, meanders, branching patterns and 120-degree joints ... nature acts like a producer who brings on the same players each night in different costumes for different roles.
>
> Peter Stevens

71 Example of student work showing an investigation into pattern. The student plays with colour combinations, shapes, motifs and orientation of the motifs to see how they work. It is playful and experimental.

Pattern has its roots in nature and designers often use nature as their source of inspiration – the zoologist D'Arcy Thompson and architect Peter Stevens explain that nature uses the same five pattern structures continuously: **branching, meanders, bubbles, explosions and spirals.**

BRANCHING Think of how the arteries in your body grow and expand or how trees grow from their roots to their outer branches. Branching patterns are seen regularly in textile design, where rooted motifs spread across the fabric surface or are constructed to form the whole.

> **An age without good pattern is an age that does not look at nature carefully.**
> Soetsu Yanagi

72 **The Strawberry Thief by William Morris (1834–1896). William Morris famously gathered his visual inspiration from nature. Morris used nature's ingredients to formulate the natural dyes that he used to print cloth and dye yarn for weaving. He revived the industrial use of the plant-based indigo dye, which is prevalent in most of his work. The Strawberry Thief demonstrates Morris' skill at creating patterns from nature.**

MEANDERS The meander is a wandering line like a long, winding river. It can be smooth and sleek and single or there can be lots of them together, giving an impression of movement. If straightened out, we have stripes. Repeating stripes is one of the simplest and most common repeat structures, particularly for knitted and woven textiles. Inspiration for stripes can be seen all around us, from clothes hanging on a clothes rail to the reflection of a landscape in water. We are surrounded by stripe structures wherever we go. Although in essence a straightforward format, getting the right balance between stripe proportions, colour contrasts and surface texture requires painstaking research. The fashion company Missoni have over many years built up their brand essentially based on stripe patterns, which can then be translated into knitwear, accessories and interiors.

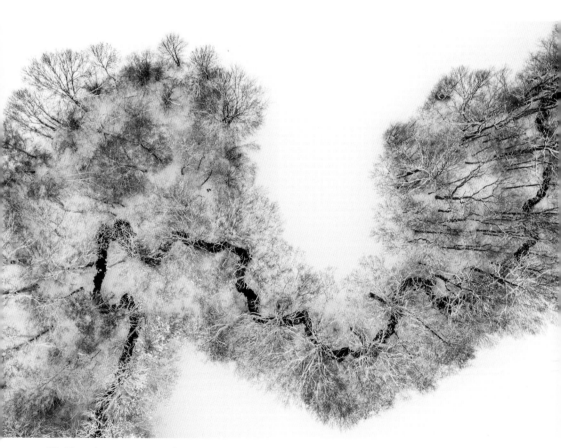

73 Meanders are present in many natural phenomena, such as the inside of flower bulbs, the human brain and flowing rivers where meanders are prevalent. It is easy to see how the constraints of growing living things cause them to wind into themselves and 'meander'.

BUBBLES Think of the way a corn on the cob has bubbles sticking side by side or the way in which soap bubbles in a bathtub stick and multiply. Bubble formations create texture as well as pattern.

74 Soap bubbles describe the repeating pattern formations that connect bubble formations wit natural forms.

EXPLOSIONS Imagine a drop of water hitting a table or a dandelion head as it is about to burst from its central point. The explosion pattern is used extensively in textiles and is often recognized as simple spotted motifs or free-floating forms across the design.

75 This dandelion head illustrates the 'explosion', one of the five pattern structures discussed here. The explosion pattern refers to the spotting and floating pattern motifs used in textile design.

SPIRALS are one of the most culturally prominent symbols and they reflect different meanings in nearly every culture. The spiral represented eternity within Celtic culture, for example. Spirals can be found in many natural phenomena, such as shells, pine cones and fern leaves. They are used extensively in textiles for their flowing and curvaceous properties.

When you look closely at the man-made environment, you will start to recognize how these five pattern structures have been used in many of our designed structures and surfaces, from architecture to textiles and graphics.

76a Spirals are commonly found in shells, where the pattern and structure opens out as it reaches the edges of the shell. Try and closely observe these formations in nature, from shells to unfolding ferns, no two are the same.

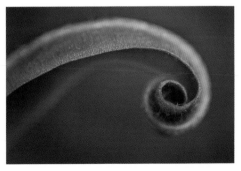

76b Spiral Aloe Vera plant, which illustrates the growth pattern of the plant beautifully.

> If pattern has a secret ingredient it lies in the skill with which the pattern-maker employs a few visual strategies ... the principles of repetition and variation.
> William Justema

MOTIFS We understand pattern as the recurrence of similar forms at regular intervals: a stripe (meander), for example, or a bubble formation. However, these pattern structures require an ornamental form that is called a 'motif' and the way in which they occur within textile design is called 'the repeat'.

Identifying a motif that could lend itself to a repeat is an essential task for the designer. Within a pattern, we can identify a single motif or a collection of motifs that are then arranged as a pattern structure in such a way as to form the basis of the design. We can refer to the motif as the core element to the design of the pattern.

While gathering visual information, it is often helpful to find the central element or motif of a repeat. Often in nature, you will find patterns that have a central form or shape, varying to some degree in colour, texture, structure and so on.

Exercise – Pattern-Generating

We have discussed the importance of pattern and some of the key components that make up pattern. In this exercise you need to think of yourself as a pattern searcher, identifying different types of pattern structures and finding the ornamental form or motif. Think of ways you might organize your motifs within some of nature's structures. This could include looking at books on a shelf, tiles on a roof or pavement patterns. Try and find less obvious patterns where a repeat element is present. Once you have found your pattern structures, capture them through drawing or using a camera. Again, think of yourself as a visual detective, trying to gather as much information as possible by looking at pattern through colour, structure, surface and texture.

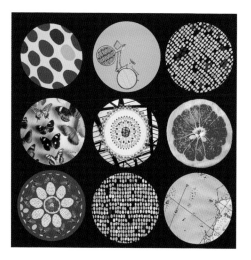

77 Student silk scarf design, showing how they created different motifs across the composition to bring repetition with variation. This combination makes the repeating structure interesting to look at.

Repeats

As previously described, a pattern is created through the repeat of a motif or motifs. The use of a repeat pattern can be seen in all areas of textile design, from wall coverings and furnishing fabrics to the fashion catwalk. Repeat patterns are extensively used within the textile industry. As a designer, an understanding of repeat is essential within all aspects of textile design and manufacture.

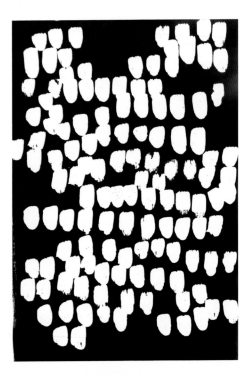

78a The student creates a random pattern derived from looking closely at birds' feathers. Sound observation at the start can give you all the information you need, whether colour, texture, surface motifs or pattern.

78b This student has used 'brick' formation to structure their motifs across the cloth surface. Although this structure is quite formal, the student disrupts it by 'flipping' the main motif to create variation.

78c This student has arranged their motifs into an abstract composition with no apparent order. It shows how the idea of an 'explosion' type of arrangement can work well as the 'randomness' creates interest to the viewer.

Disruptive Patterns

Disruptive patterns or **camouflage** patterns were originally used by the military but have now been widely adopted for fashion wear. Disruptive Pattern Material (known as DPM) tends to be inspired by the natural world and is now increasingly used by designers for cultural references.

> There are no rules, only tools.
> Glenn Vilppu

79 Student sketchbook page showing disruptive patterns being explored using the high contrasting colours of black and white for maximum disruptive effect.

What do we Mean by Structure?

Structures within fabrics come in many different forms. Some are soft, others are hard; we are surrounded by utilitarian, functional and also highly decorative and patterned structures. For woven and knitted textiles, you might consider the actual 3D construction aspects of a structure and how this can relate to your textile techniques. Woven and knitted textiles are structured fabric methods that are created through a wide range of technical processes to achieve structures and patterns. There are many structural techniques available within knitted and woven textiles that you can find in technical pattern books and online sources.

> **When it comes to structure, it is a challenge to try to pull the image out of the painting and the three dimensions.**
> Aura Wilming

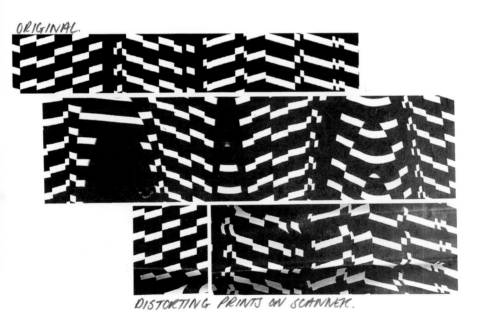

ORIGINAL.

DISTORTING PRINTS ON SCANNER.

Observing and Analysing Structure

ARCHITECTURE Unlike the body, architecture provides hard, static structures that can be used as an inspirational source for drawing. Modern buildings tend to consist of state-of-the-art materials where glass and concrete are often the most predominant. Classical architecture provides more decorative qualities, where stone-carving patterns, wooden entrances and wrought ironwork provide a different stimulus. Within every city centre, we see an array of examples of architecture. When researching architecture, it is important to remember to consider buildings under construction – even the scaffolding and exposure of the interior can provide additional structural sources.

CHAOTIC STRUCTURES Many structures around us are not organized or designed. They do, however, provide exciting examples of chaotic structures. Dishes piled up in the sink, a jumble sale, a scrapyard and a cycle repair shop are just some examples of where you may find more random types of structures to draw from.

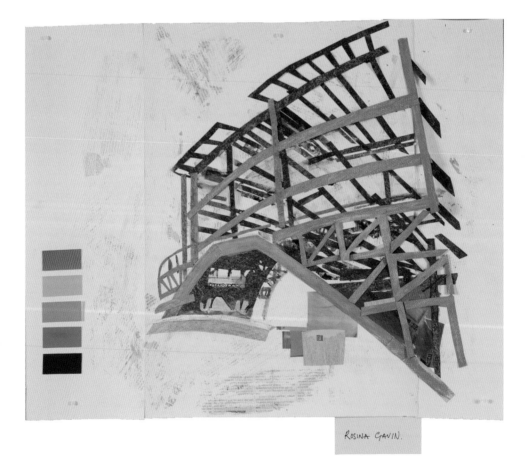

ROSINA GAVIN.

80 Student drawing using mixed media. This drawing shows how the student captured the structure of the building as it was being built to provide her with information to develop further.

81 Bottle tops discovered nailed to a wall. The rust and weathering of their colour has added to the visual appeal.

TEXTURE AND STRUCTURE Variation and inconsistency across materials can create texture. For example, by using varying widths and thicknesses of materials and line, a physical variance can be created from a monochrome drawing. There is no need to use colour. Constructed textiles, particularly weave, rely on techniques such as this when choosing the different weights, thicknesses and types of fibre and yarn to use.

In the next chapter we will explore colour from a creative and theoretical perspective, looking particularly at the importance of colour within textile design.

> Make me a fabric that looks like poison.
> Issey Miyake

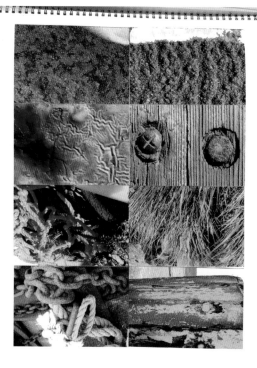

82 This page from a student sketchbook explores a number of textures in relation to one another. The student is able to analyse the different textural surfaces and work simultaneously across textures, integrating other elements such as structure, colour and pattern within their drawing.

Spotlight on Lucienne Day

Lucienne Day was one of Britain's most celebrated textile designers, known for her abstracted modernist designs that reflected the spirit of the 1950s.

She was born in 1917 in Surrey, England, and attended Croydon School of Art where she discovered her passion for textiles and Bauhaus philosophy. This philosophy advocated that artists and designers should work together for a common purpose: to produce good design that people could afford through mass manufacturing. Day was driven with a desire to create good affordable design for the many and set out to have her designs printed through manufactured outlets to make this a reality.

As an emerging designer in the 1940s, Lucienne Day excelled as a businesswoman. This was extremely unusual in an era where women were expected to manage the home and domestic activities such as childcare. Day was supported by her designer husband Robin Day, who encouraged her to promote herself and her work. She took her work out to companies to discuss sales and deals and at an early stage in her career realized that losing control of the design, the translation of the design through production, was disheartening. This inspired her to approach manufacturers differently. She would meet companies on equal terms and expect to be credited for her work as a designer. By the late 1940s Lucienne Day had established herself as a designer with her modern textiles that had a minimalist Scandinavian design flavour and clean crisp colours.

83 Lucienne Day nature inspired reproduction prints – 'Calyx' in blue together with 'Dandelion Clock'.

84 **A close-up of Lucienne Day's 'Calyx' reproduction print in a mustard colourway.**

Day was passionate about plants and flowers and is famously known for her love of gardens as a source of inspiration. She often used her garden and other gardens that she visited as a source of her textile 'motifs' which she would compose into repeat formations for printed textile designs. She often used very simple repeat structures in her work, for example, grid structures, half drops, stripes and brick formations, and it is the quality of her drawing and mark making of the motifs alongside the balance of colour that makes the designs come alive. The design 'Calyx' is probably her most iconic design, which she designed for the Festival of Britain in 1951. The 'Calyx' design depicts abstracted flowers through a series of shapes and textures, each one varying in their individual style. Spindly stems provide the vertical and diagonal lines that connect the shapes together. The result is an optimistic array of open cups that seem to blossom across the surface of the design.

In the late 1940s, with the advances of science and technology, a new way of looking at natural phenomena emerged that provided artists and designers with visual material previously unseen. The geometries of crystal structures and cells became a rich source of information for artist and designers throughout the 1950s. This future-focused approach to bringing science and design together fuelled the 'look' of the 1950s in Britain and the USA and was used extensively on homewares including textiles, furniture and ceramics. Lucienne Day was an inspiration to others and her work continues to remain so today.

Interview

Reiko Sudo

85 Reiko Sudo in her studio. Photo by Kosuke Tamura.

Reiko Sudo is Co-founder and Design Director of the Nuno Corporation of Tokyo, which is recognized as one of the world's most innovative textile companies. Nuno takes inspiration from traditional Japanese textiles, exploring their unique heritage, techniques, materials and aesthetics to create contemporary design using cutting-edge technologies. Reiko, together with her team of skilled textile artisans, is at the forefront of innovation within design and making experimenting with a vast array of materials: from silk, cotton and polyester to paper and metals, and exploring unconventional processes including salt-shrinking, rust-dyeing and burning techniques. Textiles created are visually stunning, highly distinctive and unique. Many of the Nuno Corporation's textile collections are today housed within permanent collections, including the Museum of Modern Art, New York, the Victoria and Albert Museum in London and the Tokyo National Museum of Modern and Craft. There are also a series of books designed by the company as the Nuno Nuno Book series.

Where do your research ideas come from?
Things I encounter in everyday life offer hints toward aesthetic forms, which I discover intuitively.

How do you start your research?
Very basically, it all stems from living earnestly, finding enjoyment and ease in the way we live, which in turn makes work enjoyable. That's the best place to begin. In researching, I generally start with books related to a given subject. I go to libraries and bookstores, I contact experts in the field. I almost never search the internet.

Why is research important to your work?
Materials are extremely important for textile design. Unknown materials make me think about possible applications, which leads to new designs.

Can you tell me about your design process? How do you generate ideas?
Most often ideas come about in the course of talking back-and-forth on the job with technicians and artisans.

Where and whom have you worked with/for?

The textiles we make are group efforts, so developing ideas together within our own design team as well as with outside technicians is essential. Lately, we're doing many collaborations with Japanese architects and interior designers, but I also help out silk production centres throughout Japan with design advice, and, to a lesser extent, advise clothing and accessory manufacturers both in Japan and abroad.

Who or what has had the most influence on your work?

My teachers in high school, a *nihonga* painter and dyer couple. Just seeing their lifestyle and admiring the value they placed on everyday creativity.

What do you feel is the greatest achievement to date?

When my whole being is engaged in what I'm doing and I'm living in the now, that's when I feel I've achieved something. Also, when we do textile installations at museums and galleries, I always feel fulfilled with a sense of accomplishment.

Do you have any advice for those thinking of a career in textile design?

Start from what's close at hand and find something – anything – that pleases you, then just home in on what makes it special and how you can bring out that quality.

86a 'Do You Nuno? 30 Years of Textiles We Love!' A detail from the Nuno Corporation's retrospective exhibition of their extensive experimental textile work over three decades.

86b *Feather Flurries* designed by Reiko Sudo uses waste materials from poultry farming incorporating duck, pheasant and guinea hens' feathers. This handmade innovative fabric traps feathers between two layers of woven silk.

86c *Twig Gather* is an example of Reiko's use of recycling materials where the design incorporates fragments of Nuno fabrics using a traditional Japanese method of stitching called 'Tsugihagi patchwork'.

Spotlight on Japanese Textiles

At Nuno, textiles are our language, our inspiration, our aspiration. Textiles tell our story.

When we create our textiles, nature and tradition are woven with technology.

When we see our textiles, a moment of the future is glimpsed.

When we touch our textiles, they breathe and we feel at ease.

When we listen to the language of textiles, the message is beautiful.

Reiko Sudo, Founder of the Nuno Corporation

Contemporary Japanese crafts, including the textiles created by the forward-thinking textile company the Nuno Corporation (see interview with Reiko Sudo), take inspiration from the rich cultural heritage of Japan's highly skilled artisans where craft skills have been passed down from generation to generation. Their textiles as described in the quote by Reiko Sudo express both their history and their relationship with the natural environment, which are still integral to contemporary textiles from Japan. The most famous without doubt and most widely known globally is the silk kimono with its textile patterns, an iconic emblem of Japanese textiles and their culture. The kimono has and

87a A highly elaborate silk kimono from the eighteenth century decorated with embroidered mythical Japanese phoenixes, known as the Hoo-o birds, a symbol of the Japanese nobility. Kimonos such as this one were highly patterned and embroidered as a manifestation of the wealth and power of the imperial household during the Edo period.

continues to have a high cultural value, where it historically has always been associated with wealth and nobility as an outward expression of personal standing and status.

The Kimono – The kimono dates back to the Edo period (1615–1868) where the T-shaped garment was an expression of the personal wealth of the country's most affluent. Using luxury materials such as crepe silk and metallic threads, the kimono's textiles included some wide-ranging textile techniques such as tie-dye and relief printing, together with elaborate hand embroidery. It was only in the late nineteenth century that the word 'kimono' was adopted, and through the development of the industrialization of the textile industry new silk techniques made them more widely available. The possibilities made available through jacquard weaving and chemical dyeing saw a rapid development not only in the complexity of kimono textile patterns inspired by Art Nouveau and Art Deco movements in the West but also the availability of the kimono in Europe. These vibrant kimono styles still remain popular today internationally as an iconic fashion statement symbolic of the Japanese way of life.

The history of textiles in Japan also includes a far more extensive range of textiles, techniques and fabrics than just the kimono. Prior to industrialization it was only the wealthy who could afford to own hand-crafted silk clothing. Most wore cotton and hemp textiles and furnished their homes with handmade, often recycled, utilitarian textiles. Many specialized textile techniques of dyeing and stitching have been developed within Japan and are now more widely seen in contemporary textile collections.

These include:

Indigo Dyeing – Indigo dyeing, with which we are today so familiar, particularly within the denim industry, was a popular and widely used dye method in Japan going back to the fifteenth century. The process of making the dye from indigo plant weeds and fixing the dark blue dye to cotton was developed so that through wear and washing the fading process created an enormous variety of indigo shades. The use of indigo textiles had a specific significance to the oceans around Japan, which was important both culturally and economically, and was also believed to be a natural insect and snake repellent. It became favoured by agricultural workers for these properties.

Boro – *Boro*, meaning 'tattered rags', was a form of recycling indigo-dyed cotton fabric, both clothing and bedding, to create aesthetically pleasing new patchwork fabrics using *sashiko* sewing, a decorative hard-wearing stitch technique, as a way to extend their

87b A highly skilled Japanese indigo dye artisan inspecting the fabric during the dyeing process.

normal life cycle. This repair process of 'make do and mend' today is highly popular as a designer's tool and can be seen in the work of many contemporary textile designers concerned with a new approach to creating new textiles from second-hand or worn materials. *Boro* textiles were a reminder of Japan's diminished global status after the Second World War and lost their cultural value. However, today, *boro* textiles are highly prized both by the Japanese and international market as a symbol of their history and culture.

Shibori – *Shibori* is one of the oldest indigo-dyeing techniques dating back to the Edo period (1615–1868) when the use of indigo-dyed cotton textiles was most commonly used. It is a method of dyeing through binding small areas of cloth using silk or cotton threads to isolate areas to dye, similar to tie-dyeing. The cloth can be manipulated in a variety of ways, such as stitching, crumpling and twisting, where the Japanese term *shibori* literally means to 'wring, squeeze or press' prior to being immersed in dye. Contemporary Japanese designers such as Yohji Yamamoto and Reiko Sudo continue to innovate using this ancient Japanese dyeing method.

87c An exhibition of cotton *boro* textiles showing the patchwork utilitarian clothing and sleeping kimonos worn by Japanese workers during the nineteenth and early twentieth centuries. These rare garments are now highly sought after as collectors' pieces as they encapsulate a period of Japan's history.

87d Stella McCartney's Spring/Summer womenswear collection 2019 shows how the influence of traditional Japanese techniques such as indigo dyeing and *shibori* continue to influence contemporary textiles and fashion designers.

Case Study
Wallace and Sewell

Design duo Wallace Sewell's signature design work captures perfectly the five key areas that we have discussed in detail in this chapter, namely surface, texture, pattern, structure and colour. Their use of these fundamental elements is instrumental in their unique personal approach to textile design, as seen in their work in this case study.

Harriet Wallace-Jones and Emma Sewell of British textile design studio Wallace Sewell unite craft and manufacturing – the design process starting as hand-woven samples and paintings, before being manufactured in the north of England; fusing tradition with state-of-the-art technology. They are known for their striking and often unusual colour palettes, combined with bold compositions and complex woven structure.

88 '**Erno' lambswool throw. Exploring composition and colour through the interplay of warp and weft.**

89a and 89b **London Underground wool velvet 'moquette'. Inspired by Russian constructivist textiles and incorporating four London landmarks in a small repeat.**

In addition to creating new collections of scarves and throws each year, they are guest designers for international brands and regularly create scarves tailored to key exhibitions for major galleries such as the Tate, London. They have also designed many of the fabrics for Transport for London, including the Underground, Overground and Crossrail systems.

90a and 90b Lambswool 'Transport' scarf, for the Japanese market. Abstractly interpreting Emma's drawings, through pattern and colour.

91a and 91b Lambswool 'City' scarf, for the Japanese market.

92 Fine wool 'Festival' scarf. Woven in fine wool and loop mohair in contrasting woven structures.

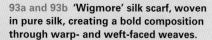

93a and 93b 'Wigmore' silk scarf, woven in pure silk, creating a bold composition through warp- and weft-faced weaves.

94 Emma and Harriet with woven lengths at the mill. Finished fabric ready to be cut into lambswool throws.

Colour

4

The Importance of Colour in Textile Design

Colour in textile design is one of the most important design elements, and learning to work effectively with colour is an essential skill for the designer. Colour can be very subjective and can come from a number of different starting points where you develop your own colour palette originating from your visual sources. As we observe and analyse these, we need to find the right methods for capturing a particular type of colour, contrast, tone and proportion. Designers are often provided with a particular colour palette to reflect a client's colour story or season. Working on interior projects, the use of colour might be predetermined by the architect or by an existing colour scheme. The context for your textile collection will also be a major factor in how you work with colour.

95 Bright colourful *gulal* (powder colours) for the Hindu festival of Holi, also known as the 'Festival of Colours'; Hindus celebrate the arrival of spring by covering one another in a multitude of rainbow-coloured powders.

96 Sources of colour can be found all around us. The material surface and reflection of light will have an impact on the quality of colour. From a simple image of balloons, we can see how light and shade create numerous colours and shades.

What is Colour?

Scientifically, colour is simply pure light, made up of the colours that we see when light is fractured, as in a rainbow or through a prism. We are able to see, compare and sense a vast array of colours and we respond to them in different ways. The scientific theory behind colour is an extensive subject in its own right, where the logic of colour in terms of its hue, saturation, tones and shade can be understood using pre-arranged sequences and systems, which in this chapter we will discuss alongside its importance to textile design.

Colour Theory

Colour theory is a set of rules and definitions that are used to understand how colours are made and work together. Colour is divided into three main primary colours of red, yellow and blue, and three secondary colours of orange, green and purple. These are then further sub-divided into tertiary colours that are mixtures of all of the above in certain orders. These create a colour wheel that we can use to explore colour relationships. The colour wheel can be divided into warm and cool colours: where warm colours are vibrant and energetic and cool colours are calming and soothing. White, black and grey are considered to be neutral.

The colour wheel is made of 12 basic hues.

These can be broken down into:

Primary – 3 (red, yellow & blue) colours
+
Secondary – 3 (green, orange & purple) colours
+
Tertiary– 6 colours created through mixing of both primary & secondary colours

Primary
3 (red, yellow & blue) colours

Secondary
3 (green, orange & purple) colours

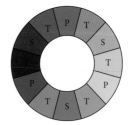

Tertiary
6 additional colours created through mixing
of both primary & secondary colours

---

97 Colour wheels.

Colour wheels, as seen in graphic computer software, are useful tools for examining the mixtures of colour that can be made.

In addition to understanding the basic colour models, it is important for the textile designer to remember that colour will appear differently when on fabric to how it appears on screen.

Colour Definitions

Colour variations can be explained by a set of definitions.

Hue

Hue means colour. When a colour is at its strongest and has not been diluted with black or white, it is at its purest. The colour wheel contains pure hues – colours with no addition of white, grey or black. When mixed with another colour of the same intensity, it remains at its strongest.

Saturation

Saturation refers to the colour intensity. A highly saturated colour contains no white and is made up of a pure colour.

Chroma

Another word used to describe the saturation or intensity of a colour.

Monochrome

When only one colour is being used, we call this working in monochrome. This is where a single colour is used, exploiting all the tones available within it.

Tone

Tone refers to the degree of lightness or darkness of colour, varying from the bright white of a light source through to shades of grey to the deepest black. How we perceive the tone of a colour also depends on its actual surface and texture. Value and shade are also used to describe tone.

Tints

Tints are shades of colour and are usually pale in nature, containing a large proportion of white.

Colour Palette

A colour palette is a group of colours selected from the colour spectrum that have been identified together within a design.

> **Look! Who says that there are only colours? There are also shades!**
> Diana Vreeland

Pure hue

Tints

Adding white to a pure hue

Shades

Adding black to a pure hue

Tones

Adding grey to a pure hue

98 Hues, tints, shades and tones.

These four basic parameters – hue, tint, shade and tone – enable us to recreate a multitude of individual colours. The colours we are able to make here form the colour spectrum where the scope of your palette will depend on your intended outcome. When you are selecting your palette, it is good to start with the colours nearest one another within the tints, shades and tones scale.

Colour Forecasting

Colour forecasters analyse a broad range of historical data and emerging developments involving political, cultural, fashion and environmental information, to name just a few, to try to predict the future trends in colour, usually two years ahead. Their work is often intuitive and they operate as zeitgeists to try and understand which colours and palettes will be important. Their insights are highly sought after by a variety of industries, not just within fashion and textiles but also by the product, automotive and graphic sectors. There are a number of websites and reference magazines such as WGSN and Trend Tablet that provide customers with up-to-date trend information. Some of this information is available online for free, but mostly customers pay a membership fee.

99 A student sketchbook that shows collected information relating to colour analysis. Students look at prediction companies for information regarding colour analysis, particularly if they intend to work in the textiles industry after graduating.

> The key is to look around you at what's happening in the design industries (and society as a whole, from politics, to tech to social unrest, to tech detoxes and a return to nature) to see how this is influencing people's attitudes towards colour.
>
> Jane Monnington Boddy, Wgsn Colour Director

100a **Student sketchbook pages showing colour analysis from source photography. The student is mixing paint to explore combinations for reds and yellows.**

Observing and Analysing Colour

Analysing colour has to be one of your paramount concerns. As discussed earlier, we see thousands of different colours with the naked eye and our job as textile designers is to reflect this enormous range of colour available to us. A Pantone shade or the colour of a crayon or gouache is a generic colour. Everybody can have access to that particular pigment or shade. Your job is to use it in a creative way to reflect the colour that you see with your own eyes.

Paint should always be blended unless there is a reason for using colour directly from the tube. Making up your own palette may take time, but will create your own bespoke colour range that only you can replicate. Take time to do this whilst constantly observing and analysing the colours in front of you.

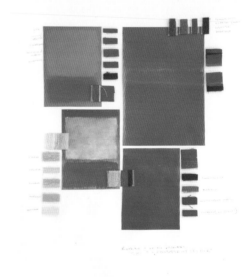

100b **Student sketchbook page with contextual research that examines Mark Rothko paintings. The student is using this as a starting point to try yarn wrapping for colour and textural combinations. This helps them understand how the cloth might look so they can make samples.**

Defined Palette and Colour Systems

There are a number of colour systems that you can refer to when creating your colour palette; however, it is vitally important when using these that you are always questioning the translation of a particular colour combination against your own visual language and design considerations and that they are balanced throughout.

As with pattern, structure, texture and surface, we rarely see one element in total isolation. Colour needs to be observed and analysed in relation to other elements that are present where they will have an impact on the intensity, purity and quality of the colour. Texture will create different densities of colour within a surface, while pattern will create repetition and variation of colour. Surface may transform colour through reflective light; structure again will transform colour by creating different perspectives, which will affect the quality of colour. All of these must be considered if your research for textiles is to be highly visual and creative.

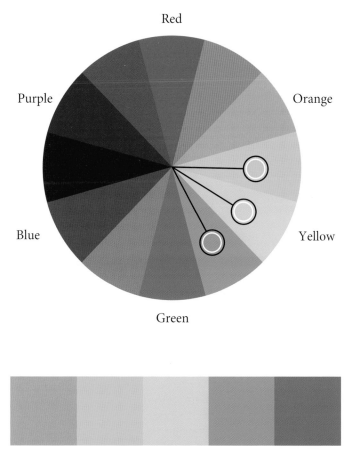

101 **Analogous palette – analogous colours sit adjacent to one another on the colour wheel where the complementary transitions are small; this gives a subtle outcome providing harmony and balance.**

Exercise – Colour 1

Take a small area (50 x 50 mm) from a selected drawing or photograph where there is an area where two colours sit adjacent to one another on the colour wheel.

Through analysing and observing these colours create a palette by mixing paint to allow the colour to migrate from one colour to the other in incremental stages.

Make a ten-colour stage palette from one to the other. You may find doing this as a stripe rather than in squares helps to see the subtle transition from one to the other.

A monochromatic palette focuses on a single hue and uses tints, shades or tones that support one another. Monochromatic palettes are useful when starting to understand how to work with colour; you are limited to one and can slowly alter the amount of black and white to add to your chosen hue to create a strong effect.

102 **Monochromatic palette.**

Exercise – Colour 2

From your visual sources in the Develop phase select a dominant hue colour that you feel reflects your context well.

Experiment with creating a monochromatic range of complementary hues simply by altering the amount of black and white that is added.

Try to create a minimum of five different hues.

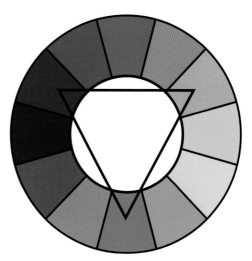

103 **The triadic colour system.**

Working with Contrasting Colour Systems

Contrasting and complementary palettes – contrasting colours are separated by other colours on the colour wheel. The more distance between colours on the wheel, the higher the contrast – these are called complementary or clashing colours. They provide impact and visibility, and can be used together to great effect.

Variations of contrasting colour combinations are the triadic, split-complementary and square and rectangle (tetradic) colour systems.

Triadic – A triadic colour system uses colours that are evenly spaced across the colour wheel. They tend to be quite vibrant, even when using pale or unsaturated versions of your selected hues. It is important to create harmony and balance here, allowing one to dominate while others provide accent.

Exercise - Colour 3

From your drawings or photographs in the Develop phase select three contrasting colours that you feel reflect your context well and relate to the triadic system principle.

Try making each of these colours the dominant in turn and the other two as accents. A tip here is to make the dominant a square and the accents a stripe.

Decide which combination creates the most harmonious arrangement and visually communicates your ideas and concept effectively.

You can adapt this exercise to all of the colour contrasting systems simply by selecting three or four colours to work with.

Split-complementary – A split-complementary colour system is similar to the complementary system and is a good place to start your investigation with colour where in addition to your base colour it also uses two colours adjacently opposite. This system provides a strong visual contrast but is less harsh.

Rectangle (tetradic) colour system – The rectangle or tetradic colour system uses four colours arranged into two complementary pairs. This system offers a broad range of colour variations. Again, similarly to the triadic colour system, it works best if you let one colour be more dominant whilst considering a balance between warm and cool colours within your design.

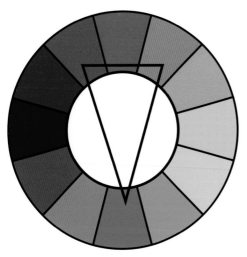

104 The split-complementary colour system.

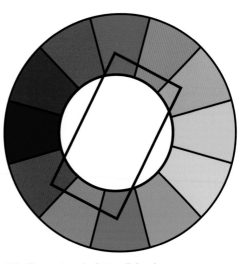

105 The rectangle (tetradic) colour system.

Square colour system – The square colour system, although similar to the rectangle, uses four colours that are evenly spaced across the colour circle. Again, it works best if you let one colour be the dominant whilst considering a balance between warm and cool colours within your design.

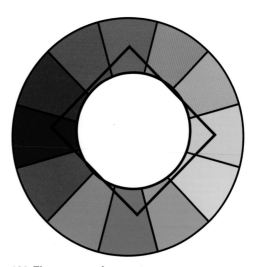

106 The square colour system.

Colour and Culture

As humans, we have very strong cultural and emotional relationships with colour. Interpretations of colour can also differ widely from culture to culture, reflecting both the contemporary and historical identities of both individuals and groups within society.

Some common colour connotations are listed below.

RED symbolizes passion, fire, blood and desire and is associated with energy, war, danger, strength and power. It is widely used for declaring love or rage. It has very high visibility, which is why stop signs, stop lights and fire equipment are usually painted red. Red lights mean stop, but 'come on' in a red-light district. In Eastern cultures, red symbolizes happiness.

BLUE is even more contradictory. Blue is for sunny sky and calm sea, serenity, peace and space. Blue is cool. Blue is quality, blue blood, blue chip. Blue is horizon, nostalgia and expectations of those blue yonders. Out of the blue comes inspiration or disaster. Blue is mouldy, blue is cold and when we get the blues we are really down.

YELLOW is sunshine, summer and growth. A warm colour, yellow (like red) has conflicting symbolism. It can mean happiness and joy but also cowardice and deceit. It is highly visible and is often used for hazard warnings and emergency vehicles. Yellow is cheerful. For years yellow ribbons were worn as a sign of hope as women waited for their men to come marching home from war.

107 Red lanterns used during the Chinese New Year, a symbol of a new beginning, bringing happiness and prosperity.

108 Blue denim jeans laid out to show the colour variation in each pair.

109 Yellow is often used in signage as a hazard caution, where it can be seen and recognized from a distance.

BLACK is associated with power, elegance, formality, death, evil and mystery. Black is a mysterious colour associated with fear and the unknown (black holes). It often has negative connotations (blacklist, black humour, black death). Black denotes strength and authority; it is considered to be a very formal, elegant and prestigious colour. Black creates a sense of perspective, depth and texture.

ORANGE combines the energy of red and the happiness of yellow. It is associated with joy, sunshine and the tropics. Orange represents enthusiasm, fascination, happiness, creativity, determination, attraction, success, encouragement and stimulation. A hot colour, orange radiates the sensation of heat.

111 Theravada Buddhist monks in Thailand traditionally wear orange robes as it symbolizes light, radiance and cleanliness. Traditionally dyed saffron cloth would have been chosen as saffron was readily available.

GREEN is the colour of the natural environment. It symbolizes growth, harmony, freshness and fertility. Green has a strong emotional correspondence with ecology. Dark green is also commonly associated with money. Green has great healing power. It is the most restful colour for the human eye; it can improve vision. Green suggests stability and endurance. Sometimes, green denotes lack of experience. Green, as opposed to red, means safety, and is the colour of 'go' in road traffic systems.

110 The black Dr Marten boot is a fashion icon and mode of dress for many people across the world. It can be powerful, classic, formal, elegant or intimidating.

112 St Patrick's Day Parade where green, a symbol of Irish identity, is the required dress colour code!

PURPLE combines the stability of blue and the energy of red. Purple is associated with royalty. It symbolizes power, nobility, luxury and ambition. It conveys wealth and extravagance. Purple is associated with wisdom, dignity, independence, creativity, mystery and magic.

WHITE is associated with light, goodness, innocence and virginity. It is considered to be the colour of perfection. White means safety, purity and cleanliness. As opposed to black, white usually has a positive connotation. Whereas black symbolizes death in Western cultures, in Eastern cultures it is white.

113 **Purple is often associated with religious festivals. In the small town of Calanda in Spain, crowds dress in traditional purple costumes to play the Easter drums.**

114 **The iconic white wedding dress, here by the Lebanese fashion designer Elie Saab, is still today viewed as a symbol of innocence and purity in many cultures.**

Spotlight on Indian Textiles

The tradition of textile making is prevalent in every culture on our planet as civilizations evolved from wearing animal skins to weaving their own body coverings and building their own shelters. Textiles in India are one of the richest examples where cloth is part of the fabric of the nation, where its meaning transcends functionality. The textiles of India are part of its economic success, craft traditions, innovative practices around spinning and dyeing, customs and spirituality. In her book *The Fabric of India*, Rosemary Crill summarizes the extent to which textiles underpin Indian culture with a quote by historian Stella Kramrisch:

> Textile symbolism in India is hallowed by tradition. In the Rig Veda and Upanishads the universe is envisioned as a fabric worn by the gods. The cosmos, the ordered universe, is one continuous fabric with its warp and [weft] making a grid pattern. Hence the importance of wholeness, not only of the uncut garment, like the sari or the dhoti, but also of the cloth woven all in one piece, on which a sacred picture is to be painted. Whether as a cover for the body or as a ground for a painting, the uncut fabric is a symbol of totality and integrity. It symbolizes the whole of manifestation.

Historically, India has been a major fibre-producing continent and this still continues today. The country has a wealth of raw materials on its doorstep, both fibres and plants, for natural dyes. Cotton (which is a plant-based fibre) was harvested and spun in India from as early as 6000 BC. Other major plant-based fibres – linen, hemp and jute – were also

115a India boasts a rich history and heritage in textile production and is still one of the leaders of textile production today. The current Indian textile industry is estimated to be worth around 108 billion US dollars.

115b Pashmina is a highly regarded wool made from goat hair, produced in Kashmir. The hair is collected, spun and woven by Kashmiri craftspeople to create one of the world's finest woollen cloths.

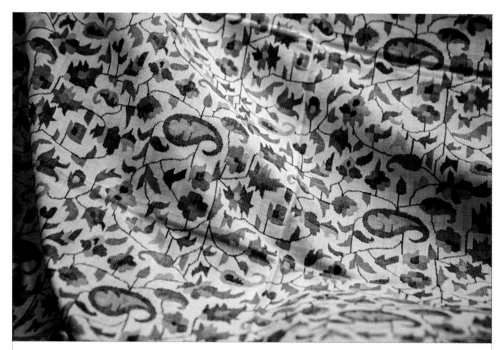

115c **Indigo dye woodblock-printed seamless Paisley pattern. Traditional oriental ethnic ornament of India, ecru on navy blue background.**

produced in abundance and contributed to the wealth of the country, as the fibres and the fabrics made from them were used for trade and gifts to curry favour with heads of state around the world. Silk (which is made from the cocoons of silk worms) was being made as far back as 2000 BC in India and the quality was rich and varied, depending on which silk worm produced the fibres to be spun. Indian silk tended to have natural beige colouring and a textured 'slub', which produced a beautiful irregularity when it was spun into cloth.

One of the most famous fabrics produced in India is 'pashmina', a very fine wool made from Himalayan goat hair in Kashmir in the most northern part of India bordering Pakistan and China. The goats that produce the hair need high altitudes to survive and the Kashmiri producers are skilled in collecting the soft hair from the herds. The hair that is harvested from the goats is so fine and light when spun into cloth; it is much sought after around the world, as it is recognized as a highly crafted cloth.

India traditionally specialized in using natural dyes on a large scale to colour threads and yarns for weaving, embroidery and printing, though today many dyes used to colour cloth are synthetic. The country became famous for the quality of indigo, a dark blue dye derived from different species of plants. The plants used to extract the indigo are native to India and the process of dyeing with indigo has been a key part of Indian textiles for centuries and a very sought-after commodity. When you look at historical examples of Indian textiles you see rich indigo blues, brilliant reds from 'Lac', a small tree-dwelling insect, red madder from plants, bright yellows from turmeric and black from a combination of various plants and the use of iron as a mordant (the substance used to fix the dye to the fibres). Together these colours are combined within woven, printed and embroidered textiles to produce some of the most exquisite textiles in human history.

Interview

Jane Keith

Jane Keith is a Scottish-based printed textile designer who is internationally recognized for her range of textile wearables, accessories and wall hangings. She is also an educator in Textile Design at Duncan of Jordanstone College of Art and Design, University of Dundee.

116 Jane looking through her dye book. All the colours that she mixes are recorded with cloth samples to build a colour library of dye recipes.

Where do your research ideas come from?
The landscapes all around. Ever inspired by where I live, surrounded by rolling lush landscapes, seascapes, colour and, most importantly, pattern.

How do you start your research?
Through drawing, observing and experiencing the landscape. The juxtaposition of colours and textures are never-ending and I take my camera and sketchbook out with me and cycle around the surrounding countryside looking for inspiration.

Why is research important to your work?
Overall, the entire design process from ideas, drawings, development, fabric sampling, application of dyes and print processes is an organic reflection of where I live, work and raise my family – the walks, the children, the dogs, the countryside, the colour, everything feeds the work and how it evolves. All of these factors are contained within the final product.

Can you tell me about your design process? How do you generate ideas?
I see pattern everywhere in the landscape. I look and see stripes, chevrons, dots, dashes, abstract composition, layer upon layer of repetition of marks and textured surfaces. These are all frequently referenced from ploughed fields, tractor trails, dried seed heads of wild flowers and weeds, fences and boundaries (both new and decayed), rolling hills of crops and forests. With each season this shifts and evolves, continuing to supply never-ending possibilities of how pattern may be layered onto cloth.

I work through the print process and see how the colours when applied to the cloth are balanced – the type of print process, the dyes, background colour and order in which the pattern and colour is applied are very important and I have to do a lot of colour testing beforehand. I usually start with white fabric and gradually build up the colour in layers. This adds depth and intensity to the pieces. Each piece is produced to the highest quality standards, in every aspect of its journey through the design process.

Where and whom have you worked with/for?

Our world depends upon sustainability, and I strive to integrate natural materials in my work. I avoid short-term disposable items as this impacts on our limited resources. Therefore, I look at how cloth is manufactured and use ethical and sustainable suppliers. I want to reduce carbon costs and I consider how the end product impacts on the global market. From a business point of view this is a continuing challenge. I feel very strongly that Jane Keith Designs, prints, processes and products should be fully contained within the UK, avoiding the temptation of

inexpensive prices of raw materials and manufacturing available abroad.

My pledge to keep my manufacturing British has advantages, however, as all of the fabrics used, such as the cashmere and linen, are hand-woven in local Scottish mills. The ties are manufactured in England, with the highest attention to detail and finish, and using the highest quality base cloth to work on. This makes a huge difference to the way in which the cloth receives and conveys colour and the patterns applied.

Who or what has had the most influence on your work?

Definitely my local surroundings and the light and colour that it produces. There is a beautiful light on the east coast of Scotland, which I try and capture within my work.

What do you feel is the greatest achievement to date?

My current body of work has seen me take the above-described influences into some new directions. I have been looking at how print lies on the cloth in relation to the shape of a garment, in the creation of simple silhouetted shapes, which can flatter and enhance the figure. Having a beautifully crafted, unique piece of design should be a staple piece in a wardrobe – whether to wear to a wedding or with flips flops on the beach. This new direction

117 Cloth fixed flat to the print table. Preparation is key as the cloth must be kept tight at all times to avoid stretching and tightening when wet and dry.

118 Oil pastel preparatory study focusing on colour combinations to inspire colour mixing with dyestuff.

has opened up new challenges, too; of learning how to draft a pattern block, and develop simple patterns with clean structural lines to complement structural print. The skirts are simple in their shape and the natural fabrics used are intended to make a dependable favourite piece which can be dressed up or down.

I am continuing to develop my cashmere scarves, which are a joy to create, the cashmere absorbing colour so easily, printing and hand painting each one to create unique pieces. I also remain faithful to my ties – the signature of the business. JKD has been producing silk ties since I started in 1997. The ties are entering a new phase, too – I am adjusting shape and construction to be more contemporary, but retaining exclusive quality that sits well with the most discerning clients. The ties seem to have been always favoured by higher-profile individuals,

perhaps because the hand-painted ones are completely unique, and the printed ties are from small batch runs – no more than twelve created at one time.

Overall, JKD is moving forward in exciting directions, whilst retaining its core values of a responsibly manufactured, high-quality, designed textile that is a direct translation of the joy I derive from the patterns and landscapes around me – and that I hope will be a pleasure to own and wear for many years, for all of these reasons.

Do you have any advice for those thinking of a career in textile design?

Yes, do it! I am a businesswoman, but I am also an educator and I see the joy that students learning textile design have when they are immersed in their subject. It's a very hands-on process which employs drawing and mark making, colour and composition, materials and processes at every stage. It is a very creative and satisfying profession … it's also hard work!

119 Model wearing a hand-printed Angora wool scarf.

120 Wool wall hanging 'Harlequin'. Hand painted and screen printed.

Case Study

Missoni

Where everyone gives you black, we still give you colour.

MISSONI is an Italian fashion house originally founded by husband and wife, Ottavio and Rosita Missoni, in the 1950s as a knitwear business. Today the company continues with an international reputation for combining craft, expertise and materials together with the latest design and colour trends. They are well known for their wide variety of fabrics in a multitude of colours and patterns such as stripes, geometrics and florals, in particular their signature graphic style, a distinctive zigzag-stripe pattern. Their knitwear collections continue to be synonymous with the brand developed through their own textile studies and inspired by twentieth-century artists such as the geometric abstract work of artist Sonia Delunay. The Italian company remains a family business, building on its rich heritage, design and technical innovation within knitwear. Their ranges have now extended into both clothing and homeware ranges.

121 **Ottavio Missoni.**

122 Missoni Menswear Winter/Fall 2018/19.

Exercise

Create a Colour Board

Using ten objects which best describe your initial RESEARCH ideas, collect a series of interesting objects that can be related by *colour, surface, pattern* or *structure*. They may come from a variety of different sources, for example your own surroundings, borrowed from family and friends and also second-hand shops. Consider your objects carefully and think about their relationship to your IDEA. What are their individual qualities and are they interesting enough? Avoid objects with logos and text and white or black. Choose objects no larger than 10 x 10 cm. Consider the following qualities when gathering your objects:

Large or small

Dark or light

Smooth or texture

Glossy or matt

Man made or organic.

Try and have a range of different qualities present in the different objects. When selecting colours, for example, 'blue', consider how far 'blue' can vary before it becomes what you might interpret as a different colour, for example:

light blue

dirty blue

clean blue

sea blue

ice blue

royal blue

blue/green

blue/yellow …

Part 1 – Using your selected objects, place them onto sheets of paper *randomly* and record them by drawing them using blocks of colour. Make sure you record any interesting arrangement that catches your eye. Record the colour combinations accurately by mixing your colours.

Part 2 – As Part 1, but this time compose your objects paying particular attention to how the objects *relate to one another*. Consider carefully your combinations and note any keywords that spring to mind that have a *'sense of your theme'*. Record the changes as you play with your objects and their colours – does the meaning change as one colour sits next to another? For example, for an IDEA exploring a theme such as MOVEMENT, keywords that might relate could be rhythmic, harmonic or the opposite meaning, such as conflicting, disharmony.

Materials required:

- craft knife
- scissors
- glue
- a variety of coloured drawing and painting media
- selection of objects
- camera or other recording media

Tips: Think whether your theme should be a cacophony or harmony of colour. Begin by blocking in colour before you add detail.Investigate materials not just on their own but in layers such as PVA glue, erasers, colour washes, conté, pastel, aquarelle, colour pencil, chalk and so on. Challenge the idea of drawing in relation to your theme and your objects.What happens if you draw using a scalpel, then take a wash of colour over the top after?

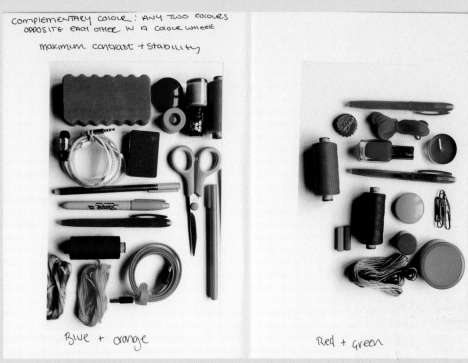

COMPLEMENTARY COLOUR : ANY TWO COLOURS
OPPOSITE EACH OTHER IN A COLOUR WHEEL

maximum contrast + stability

Blue + orange

Red + Green

123 A page from a student sketchbook where they have arranged and photographed everyday objects to explore contrasting and complementary colour palettes.

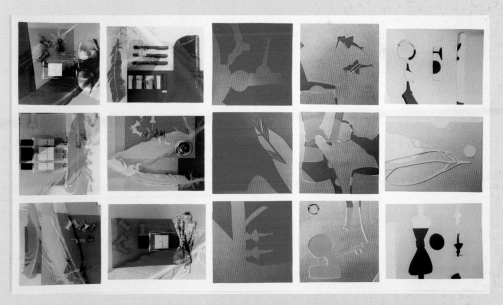

124 A student worksheet exploring the relationship between objects and colour. Here the student has developed a range of interpretations through layering and cutting techniques to create interesting colour arrangements exploring hues and contrasts.

Creating Textile Outcomes

CREATE or what you decide to create is the culmination of all your contextual and visual research. The created textile artefact is the physical making of a 'designed outcome' that has been informed by the previous two stages and demonstrates how effective your IDEA and DEVELOP stages have been through the thoroughness of your research. During IDEA and DEVELOP you will have generated an extensive body of work which now needs to be analysed and a selection made to communicate your final designs. The creation of exciting new textiles is wholly dependent on a thorough analysis of the previous stages, so it is important that you document and narrate your process and research. The sketchbook is the main tool used for this.

To get to the CREATE stage you will have trialled a variety of techniques, colour palettes and so on in the first two stages, and the final work you plan to create will reflect the previous exploration and decision-making that you have made. Therefore, the final designs should combine skilful handling of materials and a good level of craftsmanship with a 'fit for purpose' context. Material samples will be created as a collection where they come together and complement one another within your context. This stage is about making the final pieces and communicating and presenting your work to a professional standard.

125 Donna Wilson's handmade knitted 'curious creatures' are a hallmark of her brand, which she started while still a student at the Royal College of Art, London.

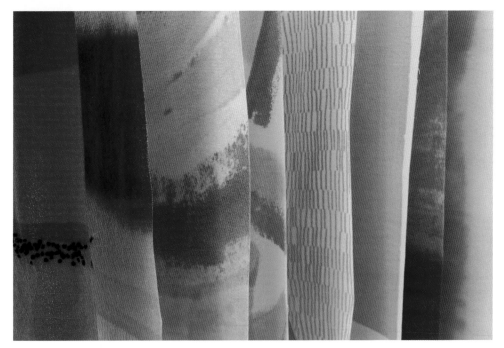

126 This student has dyed, printed and embroidered samples on wool, creating small swatches of colour and stitch before crafting their final textile designs.

It is important through the development process that you have focused on the quality of making your textiles in order that your final work is well crafted to a highly finished professional standard.

Craftsmanship

Throughout the entire textile design process craftsmanship is an essential component. Craftsmanship is often associated with historical debate, such as the Arts and Crafts movement and artisan practice, such as handmade products using traditional skills and processes. However, craftsmanship in essence comes through many hours of practising how to do something and becoming proficient at it, whether through computer-aided design technologies or hand skill. It is about developing a deep knowledge of how to do something and aspiring and being able to do it to a very high standard, in other words to do it well. Craftsmanship goes beyond traditional preconceptions of making physical objects, as it can also include songwriters, musicians, surgeons, hairdressers and runners, and it is also applicable to plumbers, bakers and butchers. All of these people have an extensive practical knowledge or area of expertise, in other words they are all crafted in their respective professions.

Within the textile design process, craftsmanship begins with drawing and working through ideas at the drawing stage. Within drawing, craftsmanship is about developing your knowledge of tools to use, colours, textures and marks that can be made in response to your visual source. The more you work on this and practice, the more accomplished you become. Essentially within textiles, craftsmanship is also applied to material development through the textile specialist areas described in Chapter 1. These also have to be learned and practised in order to gain an in-depth knowledge of the area.

Creating 'Fit for Purpose' Textiles

Creating textile designs that are suitable for the purpose for which they are designed is an essential part of the design process. Through your contextual and visual research in IDEA and DEVELOP you will have explored the types of materials and making processes that are most appropriate to use for your final outcome. For example, you may be exploring an idea that is looking at textiles for use in public transport (as seen in the Wallace and Sewell case study); as part of your research you will have discovered that the fabric must be strong and durable for long-term use. You will also have researched colour and pattern and realize that pale colours would be unsuitable, as they would need to be cleaned too often and so on. So, in order to work through this further in the DEVELOP stage you would consider yarn and fabrics qualities that require less maintenance.

127 **This student presentation board shows a well-made sample using knit and embroidery techniques. The student has 'realized' how a finished garment might look in a CAD image, so giving an indication about the end purpose/ use.**

Spotlight on Anni Albers (1899–1994)

128 'Bauhaus Imaginista' exhibition in Berlin.

> If a sculptor deals mainly with volume, an architect with space, a painter with colour, then a weaver deals primarily with tactile effects.

Anni Albers is recognized as one of the most important influential artists and designers of the twentieth century. Her work brought new meaning to one of the most important textile techniques – weave – and transformed how this medium is understood today within art, design and architecture.

As a student in the 1920s at the Bauhaus, the revolutionary school of arts and crafts in Germany, she studied hand-weaving, where she was able to develop her work both artistically as well as for industrial manufacture. As an innovating student, Albers explored the limitless grid patterns possible through weave. Her consideration of colour compositions and the tacit qualities through the construction of woven cloth continued to influence her work throughout her career.

When the Nazis closed the Bauhaus in 1933, Albers and her husband, the artist Joseph Albers, emigrated to the US and taught at the Black Mountain College art school in North Carolina, where she established her unique personal style and encouraged her students to explore everyday materials in new and inventive ways. Albers was drawn to studying the material and haptic qualities of different yarns and woven techniques to create highly textual work, where she would literally 'draw' with threads to create textiles rich in narrative. Using threads as another medium for drawing, Albers's work extended their use into woven pictorials rich with narrative.

She had a deep interest in indigenous textiles and the relationship of ancient cultural textiles, particularly those found in the South American countries of Peru, Columbia and Chile.

The textiles of ancient Peru are to my mind the most imaginative textile inventions in existence. Their language was textiles and it was a most articulate language ...

Much of her textile work took inspiration from architecture and spatial design, where she created functional work such as soundproof textile panels for large public buildings. She collaborated with architects and designers on a number of prestigious commissions, including designing in 1944 for the Rockefeller Guest House in Manhattan, New York a light-reflecting fabric as textile panels.

Later in her career Albers transferred her techniques developed through weave to print-making, where she experimented with many different methods, always sensitive to the language of textiles of colour, texture, pattern and surface qualities. She leaves a deep legacy, as she firmly believed in textiles as a powerful form of visual language. She was a strong advocate of hand-skills, recognizing the importance of balancing the use of technology with craft-making in order not to lose the qualities of textiles' unique handle of tactility and the personal expression of the maker.

Interview

Sara Robertson and Sarah Taylor

129 Sarah Taylor (Left) and Sara Robertson (right).

Sara Robertson and Sarah Taylor have been working together for four years on craft-based artistic approaches to exploring **smart textiles** through a deep understanding of material properties and the combination of traditional textile processes with new technologies. They have recently formed a business Sara + Sarah – Smart Textile Design, offering a bespoke service to enable the textile industry to innovate in the area of smart textiles and continue to work on collaborative projects that explore the creative application and artistic potential of smart textiles in different contexts.

Where do your research ideas come from?

SR: Our research ideas come through our collaboration with each other and with others. The ideas are often inspired by our work with materials, manufacture, creative dialogue and working with people from different disciplines and with different expertise. We work predominantly in the area of smart textile design and our research is often about the challenges presented with the integration of technology in soft surfaces, developing systems that allow control and interaction with these materials and transferring knowledge to industry and new markets where smart textiles have relevance beyond wearable technology.

ST: The materials and how we make them work in textiles often drive our research, for example, how can we fully exploit light as a medium within cloth and on cloth and how can we create subtle and dramatic shifts in a material surface that responds to its environment? We gain inspiration from lots of different sources, I often suggest to Sara that we go to see a dance performance and that will help us think about sound, movement, timing, space and scale in new ways. We have been working on a research project, Lit Lace for Performance, funded by WEAR Sustain. The team has included a heritage textile mill, costume and set designers, lighting designers and a choreographer to explore light-emitting lace within a theatre and performance environment. Collaborating in this way means we have to develop collective approaches to research and take on different perspectives to the research.

SR: We work together on research but we might bring slightly different things to the table. Sarah is the creative visionary one, with more of a conceptual approach, which leads our research in different directions in response to different ideas and projects. Together we seem to be able to bring things to life and make things happen much more effectively than on our own.

How do you start your research?

SR: Curiosity, intuition and **tacit knowledge** are definitely starting points for both of us. There is a trust and understanding between Sarah and myself that is hard to articulate. I would say that working in collaboration changes the approach to research as it is much more a combination of different experience, information and expertise.

ST: Yes, and this approach to research, based on our trust and understanding, allows us to be more adventurous and confident as a team. Sara is always optimistic about what we can do and that's so inspiring for taking ideas forward. We tend to start with making, prototyping, testing, for us it a very hands-on approach. We do draw, make planning sketches and diagrams sometimes, but it is more to convey a quick idea or to demonstrate to the people we are working with what we're thinking. Our research is our practice in a way, much of it is about testing new ideas, making something better, refining a process, iteration after iteration.

SR: Yes, I agree with Sarah, we do start with making and our research is materials-led, but we do also read a lot to see what else is happening in the field of smart textiles and we have to explore the context and business opportunity for the work. We do spend a lot of our time writing funding applications to progress our research and this requires a range of research methods to make sure we are able to convey originality, a systematic approach, what impact the research might have and a business case.

130 Industrially woven damask using fibre optics to create this beautiful atmospheric textile design.

Why is research important to your work?

SR: Research is our work, the research we have done in the past and are working on currently is embodied in the work we do. It is many years of knowledge and practice conveyed through prototypes/physical materials.

ST: We are moving closer to launching a new bespoke design service which will enable other people to work creatively with light-emitting lace in a theatre/performance environment. We wouldn't be at this point without a long period of research to make this feasible.

SR: It isn't without its difficulties, when involved in research you can go in wrong directions, you try methods that don't work and develop things that don't deliver what you imagined. The research process allows you to fail, it allows you to always question what you are doing and to reflect. For us it has allowed us to work with others to bring ideas to life.

131 This woven textile is designed for performance, creating a 'local' light to the performer and enhancing the drama of the interaction between the body and cloth.

Can you tell me about your design process? How do you generate ideas?

SR: Our design process is very much research-led, we are often working on research projects which are about feasibility, solving certain design problems or making something possible through integration or redesign of technology. We generate design ideas often in collaboration now – we are designing with manufacturers and our end users, in a sense we facilitate a collaborative design process.

ST: This process and the conversations involved lead us to new ideas. Looking at the fabric we make and playing with the materials gives us many new ideas. The way we take these forward depends on what opportunity presents itself. We have been very much focused on working with MYB Textiles over several years to develop light-emitting lace so our design process has been about working on the feasibility of making this happen – the design process has been collaborative, using their archive of lace designs and adapting them for the weaving of polymer **optical fibre** to maximize light and shadow in the fabric structure.

SR: We often have design challenges that we have to overcome in a short space of time. Currently we are developing the lighting and control systems for the fabric. This process is the most challenging as it is not within our expertise; however, we know what is needed but it doesn't exist currently on the market. We work in collaboration on solving this problem and we are just about to begin another iteration of the system.

Where and whom have you worked with/for?

SR: We both have dual roles in academia and as Sara + Sarah – Smart Textile Design. I work as Senior Tutor in Smart Textiles at the Royal College of Art as part of the MA Textiles programme and run our business with Sarah. I was previously in Scotland and worked at Heriot-Watt University, School of Textiles and Design, and then Duncan of Jordanstone College of Art and Design; these experiences and the legacy of smart textile research in Scotland had a profound impact and gave us the confidence to start our business. We started our business last year, so it is a very new venture for us and we've worked pretty much exclusively with MYB Textiles for several years now. We are just starting to develop work for others and with other people. We are being approached about pitching for commissions with other artists and lighting designers – this is exciting and the direction we'd like go in.

ST: In the past I have worked with designers such as Helen Storey on concept-driven projects which, at the time, allowed me to push my work in different directions for different outcomes and for different audiences. It also allowed me to work in collaboration with other teams to realize interdisciplinary work. Coming to Our Senses exhibition in 2000 led me to work with sound technologists and sensor specialists from York Electronics Centre at the University of York. This was really the start of the collaboration journey for me which over the years has led to new projects and new collaborations, for the most part, prompted through the need for technology-driven expertise. I'm a Senior Research Fellow at Edinburgh Napier University and started my research journey at Heriot-Watt University as a research student and then as an academic involved in practice-led research.

132 Colour and light are combined in this woven piece to create a sense of movable draping cloth that creates atmosphere.

Who or what has had the most influence on your work?

SR: Scotland and Sarah. I did my PhD in the area of smart textiles at Heriot-Watt University, School of Textiles and Design; that experience really shaped how I approach research and working with Sarah has been so refreshing and inspiring.

ST: Thanks, Sara! In response to that and as a model research student, Sara was inspiring as someone, who at the time, was starting to shape how PhD by practice in this area could be shaped. Her collaborative ethos was also second to none. During my time at Heriot-Watt I worked collaboratively across subject disciplines and worked closely with colour chemist, Prof. Bob Christie, to supervise design-led technology projects like Sara's. I think my first experience with the University of York had a significant impact on working collaboratively and across subject areas.

What do you feel is the greatest achievement to date?

SR: This is difficult to answer. I tend not to think about achievements. Starting a business with Sarah has been brilliant. We are focused on making this work and it gives us a sense of freedom that you don't necessarily get when working in academia.

ST: I agree. That and working with MYB Textiles and for them to be able to weave optical fibre on a large scale. Obviously, there's some way to go yet.

Do you have any advice for those thinking of a career in textile design?

SR: You are the drivers of change, training in textile design gives you such a breadth of skills and knowledge – you will not be short of opportunities but it is about finding your path. Both Sarah and I have had unconventional textile design careers – we both moved more towards research as it allowed us to continually ask questions. You may not even be able to imagine the types of work or projects that you may end up doing. I am currently involved in research that involves designing for nuclear decommissioning operators through my academic role. Recently in the media we have seen an article about the lack of dexterity of trainee surgeons – the lack of hand-skills in education is becoming a problem in all sorts of careers. These skills offer a different way of solving problems – nurture them, hone them and use them to make a difference.

ST: Our textile design training was critical to our development and a way of thinking, a way of solving problems, a way of thinking about the more technical and scientific aspects of our work, a way of embracing tools and processes, a way of designing experiments and a way of continually refining ideas. Sara's right in that the breadth of training you can get will open all sorts of opportunities. This knowledge of making and material understanding will be critical going forward for many future developments, like smart textiles for example, which is estimated will see market growth of 7 billion dollars by 2023.

Can you tell us about your collaboration and what makes it successful?

SR: Trust, balance, an unsaid understanding, respect and working together through tough deadlines, late nights and over weekends.

ST: Absolutely. And because we have fun even when it's tough.

How to Communicate

Once you have completed your development you will need to select key pieces that, in your opinion, best represent your abilities and ideas. You need to be prepared to communicate how you are planning to translate these into final textile outcomes. This might be for a number of reasons. You might need to present this, for example, for an assessment or for an interview for a course or design job, or simply to update your portfolio. Presentation and effective visual and verbal communication skills are key for every designer. Preparing to present your work is often the first opportunity to review all the work you have done so far. It is an opportunity to reflect on what you have achieved, a time to consider what to do next and to learn new skills of visually presenting and talking about your work.

Visual Presentation

Visual presentation is essentially about preparing your work for other people to view. This can be for an interview, a course or module assessment, a review with tutors and peers or simply a point at which you update your portfolio in the same way that you might update a CV or résumé. It is very important to keep a record and document all areas of your design process – both in annotated and visual form. If you start this from the beginning of the process, it makes life much easier. You might need to present or prepare your work at short notice, and having this at least partly prepared can save an enormous amount of time. In time, you will build up a range of information for presentation – visual and written – that enables you to respond effectively to any situation.

133 Student sketchbook pages showing documented ideas with fabric, colour and pattern ideas for development.

Presentation Boards

Presentation boards help to visually present your ideas in a clear and professional manner. They should be able to communicate effectively through careful selection and position your designs within a clear context. Preparing boards can be an iterative process where through trial and error and feedback you are able to communicate your thinking well to a wide range of audiences, some of which may be non-textile experts.

How to Create your Presentation Boards

Presenting your work essentially means mounting your drawings, inspiration, photographs and any other workings onto boards. The size of board will depend on the size of your piece for mounting and whether you are mounting more than one piece of work on the same board. If possible, you will want to mount your work on the same weight and size of board to keep a uniform, clean and easily 'readable' body of work together. Remember that the board needs to communicate effectively. Keep your mounting simple. Always use a white card unless you can really justify the need for a different colour, for example if your work is predominantly or all white you will need to contrast this. It is important that the board allows your work to speak for itself without being overly cluttered. Choose either a good quality white cartridge paper or thin white card. The higher the quality of board, the better the work will look, but it doesn't need to be the most expensive. Don't choose a heavy board as you must remember that you will need to be able to carry your portfolio with a number of mounted works.

Float mount onto plain white cartridge paper or thin white board. This means laying your work on top of the board. Do not cut out a frame or box mount. This

134 Student presentation board showing a collaged image of laser-cut textiles and suggested context.

rarely looks good. Remember to carefully consider where to place your visual research on the board. Always start from the centre. Mark out with a pencil and ruler where you will finally position pieces, making sure that everything is straight. If you are using any text on your board, make sure it is word-processed with a font style and size that is simple, relevant and doesn't overshadow the work.

You can fix your work to the board using either a mounting spray or tape (double-sided or masking). The advantage of using a mounting spray is that you can reposition and remove pieces easily. Be careful where you spray, though – make sure it is in a well-ventilated area. Colleges will often have a specific area for this and will not allow this to be done anywhere else. Using double-sided tape will enable you to easily move work for presentation elsewhere. Make sure that no tape is showing on the front.

Any work using charcoal, chalk pastels or soft pencils needs to be fixed to prevent smudging. Fixative sprays or aerosols can be used for this purpose but, again, this needs to be done in a well-ventilated area. If necessary, you can always place a sheet of white tissue paper over the top to prevent other boards from being marked.

How to Create a Portfolio

A portfolio is a body of visual work that represents what you have achieved so far. Your portfolio will contain examples of your most successful work, including carefully finished and presented textile samples. It will also represent your approach to solving design problems, demonstrating your drawing and visual skills and your ability to think laterally. A portfolio also includes sketchbooks and notebook work that enables a potential client or course tutor to understand how you solve problems and think through design. Not every piece of work needs to be fully resolved. Your portfolio represents you – make sure that inside and out it reflects this well. It doesn't look professional if you have beautiful creative work in an old scruffy case. When the contents start looking even slightly tatty, make sure that you remount your work.

Your portfolio is contained within a large, flat case suitable for carrying a number of loose sheets of paper. Portfolio cases can be bought in most art supply shops and vary in size from A1 (D) to A4 (A (letter)). You will probably want to start with an A1 (D) or A2 (C) portfolio.

135 **Presentation of your work is very important. Keep mounting simple and mounts or mounting boards neutral in colour. White is usually best.**

Author Tip

Mount your work on standard white paper or lightweight card.

If you need to cut paper to size, make sure that it is uniform, square and has clean edges.

If mounting visual research with textiles, do not glue textiles down – they cannot be easily removed or remounted.

Do not smudge spray mount onto photographs – it looks terrible in daylight and collects dust.

CAD Presentation

Computer Aided Design (CAD) is an important presentation tool; it is useful for many different types of presentation and when used well can create a highly professional presentation. Work can be photographed or scanned directly so aspects of it can then be manipulated. You might want to show different colour variations or changes in size, or you might want to demonstrate how an area of your visual research can create a pattern or a repeat. You may also wish to add text directly onto an image or drawing.

The results will often then be printed out using a colour printer on good quality photographic or print paper for mounting. Sometimes, however, you may be required to send off your work for a job or college application. In this instance, make sure that your images are of the highest quality. It is important to save and title your work with your name and

order your work to ensure that the external viewer examines each piece in the correct order.

Verbal Presentations

PowerPoint presentations and other digital presentation platforms are now often used to simultaneously show and talk about your work. Being able to visually present your work requires one set of skills, whilst talking about and articulating your work requires quite another. Many people do not like the idea of talking to an audience. There is, without doubt, often a certain degree of anxiety for everyone in this. Remember that you are not alone. Being able to talk about your work, to express yourself and your ideas, is an important skill that you will find you can transfer to other situations throughout your life. It is a skill that we can all learn – practice, planning and plenty of preparation will help to build your confidence.

136 Preparing and delivering verbal presentations can help you clarify your thoughts and communicate your future ideas to others. Think through what you will say and use your visuals to talk around.

Check that everything works technically and run through your presentation beforehand. Make sure that you know exactly what you want to say about each slide and be careful to keep within the time allowed. It is also perfectly acceptable to use your actual portfolio work or presentation boards to talk around. Just remember to keep everything organized so you have a smooth transition through your talk.

Creating PowerPoint types of presentations are in themselves design challenges. The overall look of your PowerPoint presentation needs to reflect your own individual style and present your work as well as possible. Be careful to avoid the numerous special effects and predesigned templates in a PowerPoint application. Keep it simple. Remember, the same rules apply as for your board presentations.

Plan what you are going to say for each slide. Keep simple notes as triggers and try not to read directly from a sheet. Remember that you need to talk to your audience, so engage with them and look at them. By watching others, you will begin to know what works for this type of presentation. Finally, remember to keep within the time slot that you have been given by making sure that you practice and rehearse beforehand.

Author Tip

Look and act like a professional. Everyone will have confidence in what you say.

Make sure that everyone can hear you.

Make eye contact and make sure that you engage with everyone.

Do you need to introduce yourself? Does everyone know who you are?

Always start positively.

Check how long you have available to talk.

Throw away all of your notes and rely on good cues on small hand-held cards instead.

Remember, you know your work better than anyone else.

At the end, ask if there are any questions.

Online Presence

The majority of textile designers will have an online presence, whether this is through their own individual or a collective website and/or a professional social media page. Many students will start to create their own online design presence from the beginning of their design course. It is helpful to start thinking about this early on as it will give you time to refine and explore what is the best approach for you. Blogs and online professional design directory sites also provide opportunities for you to present your work externally and to make and receive comments and to obtain feedback.

Case Study

Donna Wilson

Donna Wilson has been designing, manufacturing and distributing her curious creatures, luxurious lambswool cushions, knitwear and ever-expanding collection of home accessories since 2003. Her work has been featured in numerous publications and has been exhibited worldwide. In 2010 she was awarded the coveted accolade of Designer of the Year at Elle Decoration's British Design Awards, and has since gone on to collaborate with a number of well-known brands including LeSportsac, John Lewis and Mamas & Papas. As a forerunner of the contemporary craft movement, Donna has always remained true to her principles, using traditional techniques and natural fibres. Wherever possible, each product is made with love in the UK, by a team of skilled craftspeople. Donna Wilson's studio is based in East London, where she and her talented team knit, sew and send out products to their stockists and fans worldwide.

137 Donna Wilson.

138 Knitted Balloons
These knitted balloons in strong primary colours capture the playful and whimsical nature of Donna's work.

139 Collaboration with LeSportsac
Working with large international brands, such as the American bag company
LeSportsac, brings new opportunities for Donna Wilson to collaborate on
commercial projects and to see her design work reaching a wider audience.

140 Donna Wilson Homeware
Donna's distinctive and humorous textiles for the home here are inspired by
her love of nature and animals.

Case Study

Noa Raviv

Noa Raviv is a New York-based Israeli artist, who uses a variety of mediums to examine and reflect on the perception of the human body in the context of a **post-digital** era.

Working in the intersection of fashion, art and technology, Noa's work often combines traditional hand craft with innovative technologies such as 3D printing and laser cutting. Her work has garnered international press recognition (*Vogue, New York Magazine*, BBC, *Wired* and others) and has been presented globally in exhibitions, including at the Museum of Fine Arts in Boston, Israel Museum in Jerusalem and the Metropolitan Museum of Art in New York. Noa has been invited to speak in universities and art institutions around the world and in 2016 she was chosen to be included in the prestigious list of *Forbes* 30 Under 30 and was also selected by *Vogue* as one of the best young designers of the year.

141, 142, 143 Noa Raviv's 'Hard Copy Collection' inspired by the distortion of digital drawings. The design shown in image 143 includes 3D printing by Stratasys.

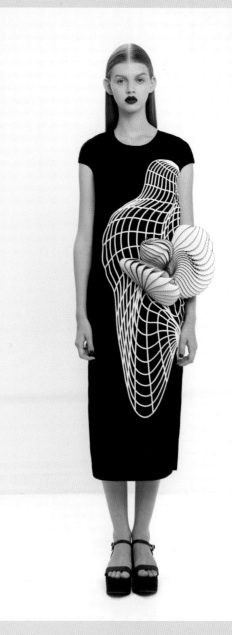

Throughout this book, we have aimed to provide you with the information and skills you need in order to undertake the textile design process. This has been based on our own design and teaching practice. The fundamental processes have been discussed and you can now apply these to your own projects. We encourage you to be as creative and experimental as possible so that you can develop your own visual language for design. It is important to constantly challenge yourself with new media and different drawing and visualization techniques. Over time, your confidence in these areas will grow and you will begin to discover more about yourself as a designer. As a dynamic design discipline, textiles are always evolving. A good designer is constantly excited and inspired by the world around them, searching out new areas to challenge existing perceptions of textile design. Do not be afraid to make mistakes. Mistakes are at the heart of creative design practice and many designers find that they are the inspiration and driving force for a new body of work. This book aims to start you on a voyage of discovery where you will learn new insights, skills and knowledge, which will hopefully inspire you to pursue a career within textile design. We wish you all the best in your chosen career and encourage you to enjoy getting there!

144 Noa Raviv, with 3D printing by Stratasys.

Abstract An idea or concept not based on reality.

Aesthetics Refers to the quality and visual appearance of an object or design.

Bauhaus The Bauhaus movement was founded out of the German school of the arts in the 1920s and 1930s where it developed a unique approach to arts and crafts.

Camouflage A pattern or design that blends into the environment.

Circular Economy Design that is a closed loop, where all materials used are reused.

Commercial Design work specifically aimed at the mass market.

Commissioned The purchase of a piece of work developed for a specific client or location.

Composition The organization of visual elements within a specified area.

Computer-Aided Design (CAD) The use of computer technology for the process of design.

Conceptual An idea that focuses on meaning as the main driving force.

Contemporary Modern and part of the present day.

Contextual Refers to information about the users of a design or product.

Craft Creative practices defined either by their relationship to functional or utilitarian products, or by their knowledge and use of traditional and new media.

Design For Disassembly The process of designing products where each component can be easily be reused.

E-Commerce Buying or selling online through the internet.

Ethical The moral principles of an individual or corporation.

Forecasting The process of predicting what the future will look like.

Mixed Media The use of more than one medium.

Mood Board A visual presentation that may consist of images, text and samples used to develop design concepts and to communicate ideas to others.

Motif A repeating theme or pattern.

Narrative A story or a series of events.

Optical Fibre A very thin flexible fibre through which light travels.

Palette A group of colours selected to work together.

Pattern Decorative forms found in nature, science and art.

Post-Digital A concept that explores our human relationship with digital technologies.

Primary Source Original material or evidence created by the person sourcing the information.

Prototype An initial sample of a design idea that is used to reflect upon before the final product is produced.

Rapid Prototyping A 3D CAD printing technique that creates samples for products ideas.

Repeat An image or motif that recurs.

Secondary Source Information that has been presented elsewhere.

Sensory Relates to the senses of touch, smell, taste, hearing and seeing.

Smart Textiles Textiles that have a digital element such as electronics or sensors integrated into them.

Sustainability Refers to the long-term maintenance of the environment, society and the economy.

Swatches Small pieces of fabric used as an example of a design.

Tacit Knowledge Human knowledge that is difficult to write down and communicated non-verbally, for example through the making or sharing of experiences.

Visual Language The method of communicating visual elements.

Black, S. (ed.) 2006. *Fashioning Fabrics: Contemporary Textiles in Fashion*. London: Black Dog Publishing.

Bowles, M. and Isaac, C. 2009. *Digital Textile Design (Portfolio Skills)*. London: Laurence King.

Braddock, S. E. and O'Mahony, M. 2005. *Techno Textiles 2: Revolutionary Fabrics for Fashion and Design*. 2nd edn. London: Thames & Hudson.

Brereton, R. 2009. *Sketchbooks: The Hidden Art of Designers, Illustrators and Creatives*. London: Laurence King.

Colchester, C. 2009. *Textiles Today: A Global Survey of Trends and Traditions*. London: Thames & Hudson.

Fletcher, K. 2014. *Sustainable Fashion and Textiles: Design Journeys*. Abingdon: Earthscan.

Genders, C. 2009. *Pattern, Colour and Form: Creative Approaches by Artists*. London: A&C.

Hedley, G. 2010. *Drawn to Stitch: Line, Drawing and Mark-Making in Textile Art*. Loveland, CO: Interweave Press.

Hornung, D. 2012. *Color: A Workshop Approach*. London: McGraw-Hill Jones O.

Jones, O. 2015. *The Grammar of Ornament*. Reprint edn. London: Girard & Stewart.

Lewis, G. 2009. *2000 Colour Combinations: For Graphic, Textile and Craft Designers*. London: Batsford.

McFadden, D. R., Scanlan, J. and Edwards, J. S. 2007. *Radical Lace and Subversive Knitting*. New York: Museum of Arts & Design.

Murray, A. and Winteringham, G. 2015. *Patternity. A New Way Of Seeing: The Inspirational Power of Pattern*. London: Conran.

Noel, M.-C. and Cailloux, M. 2015. *Printed Textile Design: Profession, Trends and Project Development*. Barcelona, Spain: Promopress.

Pailes-Friedman, R. 2016. *Smart Textiles for Designers: Inventing the Future of Fabric*. 2nd edn. London: Laurence King.

Parrott, H. 2013. *Mark-making in Textile Art*. London: Batsford.

Porter, J. 2019. *Vitamin T: Threads and Textiles in Contemporary Art*. London: Phaidon Press.

Tellier-Loumagne, F. 2005. *The Art of Knitting: Inspirational Stitches, Textures and Surfaces*. London: Thames & Hudson.

Wager, L. 2018. *Palette Perfect: Color Combinations Inspired by Fashion, Art and Style*. Barcelona, Spain: Promopress.

Quinn, B. 2013. *Textile Visionaries: Innovation and Sustainability in Textile Design*. London: Laurence King.

Museums

Victoria and Albert Museum (V&A), Cromwell Road, South Kensington, London SW7 2RL, UK www.vam.ac.uk

The Fashion & Textile Museum, 83 Bermondsey Street, London SE1 3XF, UK www.ftmlondon.org

Design Museum, Shad Thames, City of London SE1 2YD, UK www.designmuseum.org

Textiel Museum, Goirkestraat 96, 5046 GN Tilburg, Netherlands www.textielmuseum.nl

Musée des Arts, Décoratifs Musée des Arts de la mode et du textile, 107 rue de rivoli, 75001 Paris, France www.ucad.fr

Cooper-Hewitt, National Design Museum, 2 East 91st Street, New York, NY 10128, USA www.cooperhewitt.org

Fashion Institute of Technology, 7th Avenue & W 27th Street, New York, NY 10001, USA www.fitnyc.edu

Vitra Design Museum, Charles-Eames-Staße 2, D-79576 Weil am Rhein, Germany www.design-museum.de

Design Museum Denmark, Bredgade 68, 1260, Copenhagen, Denmark www.designmuseum.dk

Design Museum, Holon Pinkhas Eilon St 8. Holon, 5845400, Israel www.dmh.org.il

Websites

www.trendtablet.com
www.wgsn.com
www.sofaexpo.com
www.madelondon.org
www.helsinkidesignweek.com
www.nycxdesign.com
www.newdesigners.com
www.purelondon.com
www.maison-objet.com/en/paris
www.londondesignfair.co.uk
www.premiererevision.fr
www.pittimmagine.com
www.texi.org
www.craftscouncil.org.uk
www.designcouncil.org.uk
www.embroiderersguild.com
www.etn-net.org
www.ddw.nl

Index

0 Courtesy of Karen Nicol
1 The Dries Van Noten Menswear Fall/Winter 2018–2019 show as part of Paris Fashion Week on January 18, 2018 in Paris, France. Photograph Estrop / Contributor via Getty Images.
2 Manish Arora: Runway – Paris Fashion Week Womenswear Fall/Winter 2018/2019. Photo by Kristy Sparow/Getty Images.
3a Knitted samples courtesy of Megan Brown.
3b Woven scarves image courtesy of Wallace Sewell.
3c Mixed media piece courtesy of Laura Ukstina.
3d Print samples courtesy of Kitty Lambton.
4a Young male printer using squeegee in printing press studio. Leon Harris/Getty Images.
4b Cashmere Livestock Farming and Garment Production by Bodius Co. Photographer: Taylor Weidman/Bloomberg via Getty Images.
4c Courtesy of Josie Steed.
4d Courtesy of Frances Stevenson.
5 Copenhagen Fashion Summit 2018. Photo by Ole Jensen – Corbis/Corbis via Getty Images.
6 Courtesy Frances Stevenson.
7 Hand-printed cloth image courtesy of Jane Keith.
8 Premiere Vision Paris. Photo Jacques Demarthon/AFP/Getty Images.
9 Yarn image courtesy of Mhairi Abbas.
10 Courtesy Josie Steed.
11 Research image courtesy of Jasmin Ramirez.
12 Courtesy Josie Steed.
13 Photo John Akehurst, courtesy of the artists.
14 Faig Ahmed carpet. Photo by Reza/Getty Images.
15 Courtesy of the artist. Photo by Douglas Atfield.
16 FLOWER HEAD – NARCISSISTIC BUTTERFLY 2005 © Michael Brennand-Wood.
18 Courtesy Josie Steed.
19 Knitwear/Menswear courtesy of Tyree Hill.
20 Portrait courtesy of Fioen van Balgooi. www.jkimages.nl.
21 Fragments courtesy of Fioen van Balgooi. http://www.savale.nl.
22 Testing removable inks courtesy of Fioen van Balgooi. Photo by www.janneketol.com.
23 No H2O courtesy of Fioen van Balgooi.
24 Tree bark coat courtesy of Fioen van Balgooi. Photo by www.janneketol.com.
25 Amorfa. Savale courtesy of Fioen van Balgooi. Photo by www.savale.nl.
26 Removable print product courtesy of Fioen van Balgooi. Photo by www.janneketol.com.
27–30 courtesy of the artists. All photos by Douglas Atfield.
31 'Scramble for Africa' installation by Yinka Shonibare. Photo Johannes Eisele/AFP/Getty Images
32–33, 38, 44 Student sketchbooks courtesy of Molly Marchalsey.
34 Student sketchbook courtesy of Maike Herrmann.
35a Textiles in a Guatemalan Market. Photo by Paul W. Liebhardt/CORBIS/Corbis via Getty Images.
35b Japanese Textiles. Photo by Lea Goodman/Getty Images.
36 Artist's Paint Palette. Photo by: Universal Education/Universal Images Group via Getty Images.
37 Twelve Snow Crystals. Photo by Herbert/Archive Photos/Getty Images.
39 The New V&A Museum in Dundee, Scotland. Photo by Sam Mellish / In Pictures via Getty Images.
40 Drawing with photography courtesy of Claire Frickleton.
41 Detail of artist Sanford Biggers' "Lloottuuss," made with antique quilt fragments, spray paint, and tar at the "Constructed Histories" exhibition at the David B. Smith Gallery in Denver. Photo by Cyrus McCrimmon/*The Denver Post* via Getty Images.
42 Student drawing courtesy of Rosina Gavin.
43 Student drawing courtesy of Aimee Coulshed.
46 Courtesy of Frances Stevenson.
47 'Exploration of pavement surfaces' courtesy of Andrea Evans.
48a 'Re-use, Re-see Design 1' © Alyx Clark.
48b Drawing with stitch courtesy of Callum Donnan.
49 Examples of mixed media design courtesy of Lucy MacMillan.
50 Student sketchbook collage courtesy of Amy Carter.

51 Relief drawing courtesy of Eilidh Harper.

52 Observing lines courtesy of Jasmin Ramirez.

53 3D drawing courtesy of Rebecca Logue-Reid.

54 Japanese artist Yuken Teruya with one of his artworks which consists of paper shopping bags with trees cut out of the bags, part of an exhibition at the Object Gallery, 4 September 2006. SMH Picture by Steven Siewert (Photo by Fairfax Media via Getty Images).

55 Light mind map courtesy of Judy Scott.

56 Theme boards courtesy of Joy Gansh.

57 Karen Nicol in her studio. Courtesy of Karen Nicol.

58 Liberty Quilt. Courtesy of Karen Nicol.

59 Design for Schiaparelli. Courtesy of Karen Nicol.

60 Ice Bear. Courtesy of Karen Nicol.

61 Book Flag. Courtesy of Karen Nicol.

62 World map large scale art commission, Black Rock investment bank, Hong Kong. Courtesy of Karen Nicol.

63 Dries Van Noten: Details – Paris Fashion Week Womenswear Fall/Winter 2018/2019. Estrop / Contributor. Getty Images Entertainment.

64 Dries Van Noten: Runway – Paris Fashion Week – Menswear F/W 2019–2020. Photo by Richard Bord/Getty Images.

65 Student mixed-media textile courtesy of Stephanie Davidson.

66a Surface effect study courtesy of Kendall Blair.

66b Abstract textile prints courtesy of Beanie Cathro.

67 Mixed media work courtesy of Kimberley Smith.

68 Sketchbook pages courtesy of Lucy Caster.

69 Digital printing on cloth courtesy of Lauren McDowall.

70 Drawing with stitch courtesy of Kirsty Fenton.

71 Patterns student work courtesy of Maike Herrmann.

72 'The Strawberry Thief', textile designed by William Morris, 1883. Artist William Morris. Photo by Historica Graphica Collection/ Heritage Images/Getty Images.

73 Aerial view of a small river in winter on January 11, 2019 in Reichenbach, Germany. Photo by Florian Gaertner/Photothek via Getty Images. 74 Abstract colourful bubbles, oil and water. Photo by Education Images/Universal Images Group via Getty Images.

74 Abstract colourful bubbles, oil and water. (Photo by: Education Images/Universal Images Group via Getty Images)

75 Macro detail of the seed head of a common dandelion (Taraxacum officinale), taken on May 13, 2014. Photo by Claire Gillo/Digital Camera Magazine/Future via Getty Images.

76a Interior of a pearly nautilus shell. Photo by Wild Horizons/Universal Images Group via Getty Images.

76b Close-up detail of the curled tip of a young wild garlic shoot, taken on May 21, 2010. Photo by Ben Brain/Digital Camera Magazine/ Future via Getty Images.

77 Silk scarf image courtesy of Errin Miller.

78a Feather composition courtesy of Joy Gansh.

78b Brick composition courtesy of Georgina Hickey.

78c Abstract composition courtesy of Kitty Lambton.

80 Student drawing of a building structure courtesy of Rosina Gavin.

81 Courtesy Frances Stevenson

83 and 84 Lucienne Day – Dandelion Clocks and Calyx Blue (printed on Linen Union by Classic Textiles). Calyx Yellow (Printed on Linen Union by Classic Textiles). Images courtesy of Classic Textiles – www.classictextiles.com.

85 Reiko Sudo in her studio. Photo by Kosuke Tamura.

86 a, b and c 'Do You Nuno? 30 Years of Textiles We love!', 'Feather Flurries' and 'Twig Gather' courtesy of Reiko Sudo.

87a Nuihaku No Robe with Phoenixes and Branches. Photo by Ashmolean Museum/ Heritage Images/Getty Images.

87b A senior traditional artisan checking the quality of his indigo dyeing work. Photograph Trevor Williams/Getty Images.

87c "Boro – Stoffe des Lebens". Photo ullstein bild/Getty Images.

87d Stella McCartney: Runway – Paris Fashion Week Womenswear Spring/Summer 2019. Photo Estrop / Contributor/ Getty Images.

88–94 Wallace & Sewell images courtesy of Wallace Sewell.

95 Holi festival colour powder piles. Photo by Zohaib Hussain/IndiaPictures/Universal Images Group via Getty Images.

96 Courtesy Josie Steed.

100a Student sketchbook page with contextual research courtesy of Sophie MacCaffrey.
100b Sketchbook research courtesy of Claire Frickleton.
107 Red lanterns. Photo by Zhang Wei/China News Service/Visual China Group via Getty Images.
108 Jeans. Photo by: Marka/Universal Images Group via Getty Images.
109 Caution sign. Photo by Roberto Machado Noa/LightRocket via Getty Images.
110 Shoe detail at the John Richmond show during Milan Menswear Fashion Week Autumn/Winter 2019/20 on January 13, 2019 in Milan, Italy. Photo Estrop / Contributor via Getty Images.
111 Monk meditating in Wat Trahimit, Bangkok, Thailand. (Photo by: Godong/Universal Images Group via Getty Images.
112 St Patrick's Day celebration. Photo by: PYMCA/Universal Images Group via Getty Images.
113 Calanda drums. Photo by Miguel Sotomayor via Getty Images.
114 Elie Saab: Runway – Paris Fashion Week Haute-Couture Spring/Summer 2013. Photo by Kristy Sparow / Stringer via Getty Images.
115a Saree Manufacturers in Pali in Rajasthan on March 10, 2017 in India. Photo by Frédéric Soltan/Corbis via Getty Images.
115b Kashmiri artisan Shabir Ahmed (L) is watched by fellow weaver Shakeel as he uses tooji to weave a Kani or Jamewar shawl at his workshop in Srinagar, 05 March 2007. Photo by ROUF BHAT/AFP/Getty Images.
115c A pashmina shawl on display at a store in Srinigar, Jammu and Kashmir, India. Photo by Prashanth Vishwanathan/Bloomberg via Getty Images.

116–120 Courtesy of Jane Keith.
121 Ottavio Missoni in his study in 1984. Photo by Angelo Deligio/Mondadori via Getty Images.
122 Missoni – Runway – Milan Fashion Week Fall/Winter 2018/19. Photo by Victor VIRGILE/Gamma-Rapho via Getty Images.
123 Colour collections courtesy of Cassandra Humphrey.
124 Design work courtesy of Elaine Gowans.
125 'Creatures' courtesy of Donna Wilson.
126 Dyed, printed and embroidered samples on wool courtesy of Robyn Nisbet.
127 Courtesy Josie Steed
128 'Bauhaus Imaginista' exhibition In Berlin Photo by Sean Gallup/Getty Images.
129–130 courtesy of Sara Robertson and Sarah Taylor.
131–132 courtesy of Sara Robertson and Sarah Taylor. Photos by Margot Watson.
133 Student sketchbook showing fabric, colour and pattern ideas courtesy of Morgan Campbell.
134 Collage fashion illustration courtesy of Laura Morrison.
135–6 Courtesy Josie Steed
137–140 Courtesy of Donna Wilson.
141–144 Courtesy of Noa Raviv. Photography by Ron Kedmi.

All reasonable attempts have been made to trace, clear and credit the copyright holders of the images reproduced in this book. However, if any credits have been inadvertently omitted, the publisher will endeavour to incorporate amendments in future editions.

Acknowledgements

We would like to thank everyone who has so generously contributed and supported us during this project. In particular we would like to thank:

Freddie Robins, Alan Shaw, Donna Wilson, Noa Raviv, Karen Nicol, Fioen Van Balgooi, Sara Robertson, Sarah Taylor, Jane Keith, Harriet Wallace-Jones, Emma Sewell, Lucy Orta, Faig Ahmed, Reiko Sudo, Michael Brennan Wood, Elaine Gowans, Fiona Stephen, Fergus Connor, Robin Wilson, Jess Fawcett, Yinka Shonibare, Laura McPherson, Malcolm Finnie and Joe Hart.

We would also like to thank our past and current students who have provided inspiration and have kindly allowed so many images of their work to illustrate this book. We would especially like to thank:

Cassandra Humphries, Freya Aitken-Scott, Siobhan Thomson, Kirsty Fenton, Callum Donnan, Laura Ukstina, Jasmin Ramirez, Amy Forbes, Kitty Lambton, Amy Mowatt, Laura Morrison, Alyx Clark, Lauren McDowall, Stephanie Davidson, Bekki Logue-Reid, Kimberley Smith, Andrea Evans, Tyree Hill, Morgan Campbell, Clari Hayman, Judy Scott, Megan Brown, Mhairi Abbas, Maike Herrmann, Kendall Blair, Claire Frickleton, Sophie McCaffrey, Amy Carter, Beanie Cathro, Georgina Hickey, Molly Marshalsey, Aimee Coulshed, Rosina Gavin, Ellie Donnan-Thompson, Victoria Potts, Errin Miller, Eilidh Harper, Georgia Barr, Joy Gansh., Lucy McMillan, Lucy Caster and Robyn Nisbet.